EXEGESIS OF DIFFICULT PASSAGES

EXEGESIS OF DIFFICULT PASSAGES

JACK P. LEWIS, PH. D.

Resource Publications
202 S. Locust
Searcy, Arkansas 72143

ISBN 0-945441-00-2

To all
whose ideas have challenged
and stimulated my
thinking

*"Open my eyes that I may see
wonderful things in your law"
(Ps. 119:18).*

*"Doubt comes in at the window
when inquiry is denied at the door."
(Benjamin Jowett)*

Contents

Abbreviations

A. Apion — *Against Apion*
Adv. Haer. — *Against Heresies*
ANF — *Ante-Nicene Fathers*
Apol. — *Apology*
ASV — The American Standard Version
AV — The Authorized Version
CD — *Cairo Damascus Document*
F. — *Florilegium*
Gen. R. — *Genesis Rabbah*
GKC — Gesenius-Kautzsch-Cowley's *Hebrew Grammar*
JNES — *Journal of Near Eastern Studies*
KJV — The King James Version
LXX — The Septuagint
NAB — The New American Bible
NASV — The New American Standard Version
NEB — The New English Bible
NIV — The New International Version
NKJV — The New King James Version
NTS — *New Testament Studies*
QH — Qumran *Thanksgiving Psalms*
QP — Qumran *Commentary*
QS — Qumran *Order of the Community*
Q Temple — Qumran *Temple Scroll*
RSV — The Revised Standard Version
RV — The Revised Version
T.B. — *Talmud Babli*
TDNT — *Theological Dictionary of the New Testament*
TEV — Today's English Version
TLB — Taylor's *The Living Bible Paraphrased*
ZNTW — *Zeitschrift für die neutestamentliche Wissenschaft*

Bible Abbreviations

OLD TESTAMENT

Genesis	Gen.	Ecclesiastes	Eccles.
Exodus	Ex.	Song of Solomon	Song
Leviticus	Lev.	Isaiah	Is.
Numbers	Num.	Jeremiah	Jer.
Deuteronomy	Deut.	Lamentations	Lam.
Joshua	Josh.	Ezekiel	Ezek.
Judges	Judg.	Daniel	Dan.
Ruth	Ruth	Hosea	Hos.
1 Samuel	1 Sam.	Joel	Joel
2 Samuel	2 Sam.	Amos	Amos
1 Kings	1 Kings	Obadiah	Obad.
2 Kings	2 Kings	Jonah	Jon.
1 Chronicles	1 Chron.	Micah	Mic.
2 Chronicles	2 Chron.	Nahum	Nahum
Ezra	Ezra	Habakkuk	Hab.
Nehemiah	Neh.	Zephaniah	Zeph.
Esther	Esther	Haggai	Hag.
Job	Job	Zechariah	Zech.
Psalms	Ps.	Malachi	Mal.
Proverbs	Prov.		

NEW TESTAMENT

Matthew	Mt.	1 Timothy	1 Tim.
Mark	Mk.	2 Timothy	2 Tim.
Luke	Lk.	Titus	Tit.
John	Jn.	Philemon	Philem.
The Acts	Acts	Hebrews	Heb.
Romans	Rom.	James	Jas.
1 Corinthians	1 Cor.	1 Peter	1 Pet.
2 Corinthians	2 Cor.	2 Peter	2 Pet.
Galatians	Gal.	1 John	1 Jn.
Ephesians	Eph.	2 John	2 Jn.
Philippians	Phil.	3 John	3 Jn.
Colossians	Col.	Jude	Jude
1 Thessalonians	1 Thess.	Revelation	Rev.
2 Thessalonians	2 Thess.		

Apocrypha Abbreviations

1 Esdras	1 Esd.
1 Maccabees	1 Macc.
2 Maccabees	2 Macc.
3 Maccabees	3 Macc.
Tobit	Tob.
Judith	Judith
Sirach	Sir.
or Ecclesiasticus	Ecclus.
Wisdom of Solomon	Wisd.
1 Baruch	1 Bar.
Epistle of Jeremy or Letter of Jeremiah	Ep. Jer.
Prayer of Manasses	P. Man.
Prayer of Azariah and Song of the Three Children	Azar.
Susanna	Sus.
Bel and the Dragon	Bel
Additions to Esther	Add. Esth.

Pseudepigrapha Abbreviations

Book of Jubilees	Jub.
Letter of Aristeas	Arist.
Apocalypse of Moses	Apoc. Mos.
Books of Adam and Eve	Adam and Eve
Martyrdom of Isaiah	Mart. Is.
1 Enoch	1 En.
Testament of the XII Patriarchs	Test. XII Patr.
Testament of Reuben	T. Reu.
Testament of Simeon	T. Sim.
Testament of Levi	T. Levi
Testament of Judah	T. Jud.
Testament of Issachar	T. Iss.
Testament of Zebulun	T. Zeb.
Testament of Dan	T. Dan
Testament of Naphtali	T. Naph.
Testament of Gad	T. Gad
Testament of Asher	T. Ash.
Testament of Joseph	T. Jos.
Testament of Benjamin	T. Benj.
Sibylline Oracles	Sib.
Assumption of Moses	Ass. Mos.
2 Baruch	2 Bar.
4 Ezra	4 Ez.
Psalms of Solomon	Ps. of Sol.
4 Maccabees	4 Macc.
Pirke Aboth or Sayings of the Fathers	Aboth
Story of Ahikar	Ah.
Zadokite Fragments	Zad.

Acknowledgements

My gratitude is offered to the *Harding Graduate School Bulletin* for its kindness in previously publishing the articles which are here reprinted: "Pretexting?", "Predicting the Virgin Birth" (Isaiah 7:14), and "Remarriage" (1 Corinthians 7); to the *Gospel Advocate* for "The Woman's Seed" (Genesis 3:15), " 'Putting Away' and Divorce," and "A Cloud of Witnesses" (Hebrews 12:1); to Abilene Christian University Lectures, 1979, for "When a Man . . ." (Deuteronomy 24:1-4); to the Harding University Lectures, 1966, for "The Christian and the Government" (Romans 13:1-7) and the Harding University Lectures, 1974, for "The Intermediate State of the Dead"; to *The Exegete* for "The Priesthood" (1 Peter 2:5-9); to the National Christian Press, *Your Marriage Can Be Great*, for "From the Beginning It Was Not So" (Matthew 19:8); to the *Restoration Quarterly* for "*Baptizein* and *Kōluein*" (Mark 10:14); to the *Firm Foundation* under its prior editorship for "Mark Them Which Cause Divisions" (Romans 16:17), " 'Spiritual Words' or 'Spiritual Men'?" (1 Corinthians 2:13), "The Woman's Seed" (Genesis 3:15), "Living Soul" (Genesis 2:7), and "Virgin *Daughter*" (1 Corinthians 7:36-38); to *Image* Magazine for "Those Who Rule" (Hebrews 13:7, 17, 24); and to *Difficult Texts of the Old Testament Examined*, Brown Trail School of Preaching Lectures, 1982, for "Difficult Texts From the Psalms and Proverbs."

My gratitude is also to Mrs. Susan Cloer and her staff of Typesetting, Etc., for their excellent help in putting the book together and seeing it through the press. Help has been had in proofreading from Mrs. Jean Saunders and Mrs. Jane Tomlinson, secretaries at the Harding Graduate School of Religion, and from my wife Annie May. The blame for errors remaining are mine, not theirs. Publishing convinces one beyond any doubt that the time for his being declared infallible has not begun to approach.

Introduction

The miscellaneous studies which are here presented have been written over the period of many years in response to various stimuli. The majority have previously appeared in diverse publications and are here gathered with other articles in the hope that they may yet be of use to students in the study of their Bibles. One is debtor to all he has met: those from whose works he has borrowed, those contemporaries who have spoken words of encouragement at the efforts he has made, and also to those with whom he differs but whose voiced opinions have been a stimulus to him to search for a better understanding and have motivated him to expound what he sees as the truth.

The Lord delivered his Word to us through men he inspired to write (2 Tim. 3:15); however, those men wrote in Hebrew and Greek as their native language happened to be. The transmission of their words has been by the human process of copying, and the extent to which that process has been providentially guided is not a subject on which Scripture has made clear statements. Such a proposition is subject to opinion, but not to either proof or disproof. Since the manuscripts which have come to us do have variants in them, the process of textual criticism is a necessary one lest one find himself saying, "Thus says the Lord," when in reality he should be understanding, "Thus copied a scribe." People tend to identify that which is traditional with the Bible and to feel that any deviation from it is either adding to the Bible or taking from it. However, in view of the manuscript variants, the significant question is, “What is the Bible?”—that is, what did the writers write? If a phrase were without question supported by the manuscript evidence, no one would leave it out; if it had no manuscript support, no one would add it. Translations which we have had a long time are not the measuring stick of what the text should be.

The process of translating is also a human process. There is no reason to suppose that the Holy Spirit was operative at one stage of translating but now inoperative. The translators of the past claimed no infallible guidance; it is only long use of their production which causes some to feel that they must have been divinely guided.

We all read God’s Word in translation, and the most informed of us struggle with the original languages. Interpretations become traditional, but new information may show that they need to be corrected. Change of language with words going out of use, new words coming into use, and meanings being modified may cause men to understand what they are reading in a way the writer never meant. That interpretations have been around a long time is no assurance that they have been well-founded.

Men ask the Bible questions out of the situation in which they are. Often those questions were not the questions biblical writers were answering when they wrote their various books. What they said may apply to the modern situation only by analogy; but there is a pitfall which needs to be guarded against. In general when men have asked the Bible a question the writer was not answering, they merely confirmed themselves in a position they had already consciously or unconsciously taken on other bases.

A series of studies of this sort must necessarily raise some questions which the reader has not thought of before. It may bring to his attention relevant evidence which he has not had access to before. In some cases it may go directly contrary to opinions which he knows are widely held. It is hoped by the author that when appeal has been made to Hebrew and Greek, the evidence from those languages has been made clear even to the person who has not had the advantage of studying them first-hand.

Though the author has in each case set forth that of which he is convinced, he holds no illusions about his being above error. He certainly has no ideas about his having a corner on truth. He is aware that all have blind spots. Should these articles prove to be demonstrations of the beams in his eye, may those who have only motes enlighten the Lord's people in better ways.

The Word of the Lord will not return to him void (Is. 55:11). May we give the more diligence to understand what he has said! May our minds always remain open to his truth which has not yet dawned into our consciousness! May our hearts be brought into subjection to him that every thought may be taken captive to the obedience of Christ!

April 27, 1988

1

Pretexting?

The old saying that "a proof text is often a pretext" may be used as a starting point—to ask those of us who preach and teach whether we are expounding to our audiences the revelation of God or whether we are hanging our own ideas on convenient Scripture passages. The temptation to pretext is ever present in a community which feels that there must be a biblical base for all that is done in work and worship. We are not always clear about what falls in the necessary inference category for which no explicit Scripture statement is needed. The result is that we are tempted to try to find proof where none exists.

The exegetical methods of the rabbis were systematized with statable rules, but in general can be called "hanging mountains by strings." To give only one example, later codifiers, out of a saying like "You shall not boil a kid in its mother's milk" (Ex. 23:19; 34:26; Deut. 14:21), arrived at the prohibition of eating milk and meat at the same meal.

The Qumran community found the prophets describing conditions that community had to face. Their exegetical method to some extent reminds one of that of modern interpreters who find cars, airplanes, tire rationing, and Middle Eastern political problems in Scripture. The more resourceful the exegete, the more clever combinations he can come up with to impress his audience. None of it is what the biblical writers had in mind when God spoke through them.

The early church fathers had the messianic interpretation as the magical key with which to unlock all Old Testament passages. Amos' statement "in that day the sun will go down at noon" was a prediction of the darkness at the crucifixion.[1] "The Lord hath spoken in Zion" predicted Jesus' appearance in Judea.[2] In that and every age since, the allegorical interpretation of Scripture has been a means by which men claimed a Scripture base for ideas they had otherwise accepted. Augustine expounded the parable of the Samaritan as giving a picture of human history. According to him, mankind started down the road of life but fell into sin which beat him and left him helpless in the ditch. The law of Moses came and also passed him by. Finally, the good Samaritan, Jesus, bound up his wounds and brought him into the inn of safety—the church. While the basic outline of Augus-

[1]Irenaeus *Adv. Haer.* 4.33.12 (ANF 1:310).
[2]Ibid., 4.33.11 (ANF 1:500).

tine's case is true, the parable of the Samaritan does not teach it when legitimately exegeted. Augustine hung his ideas on the parable; he did not derive them from it.

Not long ago a speaker, urging the need of congregations to follow the leadership of the elders, came up with the clever turn on Judg. 5:1-2: "When the elders lead and the people follow, we will praise the Lord." The situation he described is to be desired; but I wanted to ask him if he meant to leave the impression that he was giving a legitimate exegesis of his proof passage or if he meant it as an example of his cleverness? If one has to twist a passage to support the truth he is expounding, would it not be better to omit the passage and just to expound the idea on its own merits?

An informed speaker, wishing to expound the idea that there is something mysterious about the appeal that wickedness has in the lives of a modern people, took as his proof text 2 Thess. 2:7—"the mystery of lawlessness." Anyone can see that there are aspects of wrongdoing that are not to be explained. One may know the truth and then not do it; one may know the consequences of the life of sin, but live it anyway. Who can explain it? A doctor spoke to us on the dangers of drug abuse; but doctors who know what drugs will do are often offenders in the abuse. Knowing the right and the wrong does not give one the will to choose the right and to reject the wrong. It is a puzzle to all of us—but that is an entirely different ball game from what Paul was expounding in 2 Thessalonians 2. If one has a valid idea, is a pretext necessary?

A speaker, wanting to expound his concept of the providence of God, insisted that God put base men in governmental positions and then out of their wickedness accomplished his purpose. He insisted that Hitler was a base man whom God put over the Germans. Stalin was a base man put over the Russians. The speaker failed to observe that he had misunderstood his Bible and had fallen into the trap laid by the change in meaning of English words. “Base” in 1611 meant “humble” or “lowly,” and Dan. 4:17, 25, 32; 5:21 say that God puts “lowly men” on the throne—not “base men” in the sense meant by the epithet “Mean Joe Green.” The text chosen had become only a pretext.

2

"Living Soul"

Genesis 2:7

> And the Lord God formed man of the dust of the ground, and breathed into his nostrils the breath of life; and man became a living soul (Gen. 2:7; KJV; ASV).

It is in particular the line of reasoning premised upon this verse which argues that man has a living soul and that animals do not have souls that I wish us to look at. For many people this verse in Genesis describes the one distinctive thing that makes a man different from animals. But the RSV, followed by the NASV and NEB, translated the key word of the verse as "living being" while the NEB used "living creature." Either choice radically affects the argument.

The word at issue in this passage is *nephesh chayyah*, which occurs in seven Old Testament passages and is translated into Greek as *psuchē zōsa*. Assuming that *nephesh* is "soul," then either the Greek or Hebrew could very literally be "living soul" as it is in the AV. However, the logical and linguistic opposite of *nephesh chayyah* is *nephesh meth* (dead soul or dead being), which occurs in such statements as where the priest shall not defile himself for any dead body (Lev. 21:11) and where the man with a Nazirite vow is not to go near a dead body (Num. 6:6).

It should be obvious to all that we are not here dealing with what we would ordinarily understand had our English translators rendered these passages "dead souls." Such an expression could only be understood to speak of one living in sin and thereby spiritually dead, or of one who experiences eternal death. "The soul that sins shall die," threatens the prophet (Ezek. 18:4). The lake of fire is second death.

That which has been obscured to us because of variety in our English translations is that the creatures are also *nephesh chayyah* in the passage where God says, "Let the earth bring forth living creatures . . ." (Gen. 1:24). They have in them *nishmath chayyah*, that is, "breath of life" (KJV: life), and are given the grass for food (Gen. 1:30). When the flood comes, the rainbow is a sign of the covenant with every living creature which is with Noah in the ark (Gen. 9:12). God remembers the covenant with every living creature of all flesh and will not repeat the flood (Gen. 9:15), for he is reminded of the covenant with every living creature of all flesh upon the earth (Gen. 9:16). The final occurrence of this term is in Ezekiel's description of the river flowing from the temple in which every living creature which swarms will live (Ezek. 47:9).

Only in one out of the seven passages where *nephesh chayyah* occurs is man the exclusive object of discussion. *Nephesh chayyah,* that is, man and animals, contrast in the creation picture with plants which have only vegetable life. It would seem that arguments which try to present the distinctiveness of man from the term "living soul" are actually based on the phenomena of variety in translation of the KJV and have no validity in fact. Had the translators rendered all seven occurrences by the same term, we would have been aware of the fact that both men and animals are described by it.

To make this observation is not at all to affirm that the Old Testament is materialistic. We are concerned at this time only with the biblical usage of one term. Neither is it to deny a distinction in biblical thought between men and other animals when one takes in consideration the whole Old Testament view. Man may perish like the animals, but he is different from them. Even here in Genesis in the creation account, God is not said to breathe into the animals the breath of life; animals are made male and female; there is no separate account of the making of the female animal; they are not said to be in God's image and likeness; they are not given dominion. Man is the crown of God's creation. He names the animals, and after the flood it is announced that man's blood is required of the beasts (Gen. 9:5).

The ultimate description of man's make-up is found in 1 Thess. 5:23: "May your spirit and soul and body be kept sound and blameless at the coming of our Lord Jesus Christ."

3

The Woman's Seed

Genesis 3:15

> I will put enmity between you and the woman, and between your seed and her seed [KJV; ASV; NAB: offspring; but NEB: brood]; he shall bruise your head, and you shall bruise his heel (Gen. 3:15).

Gen. 3:15, traditionally interpreted as the first Gospel, is thought by many to contain a rather plain prediction of the Virgin Birth because of its allusion to the woman's seed. While this passage is not appealed to by any New Testament writer as a proof or prediction of the Virgin Birth, early in Christianity its applicability to that question was observed, and repeatedly apologists have appealed to it. The strong point of the argument is obviously the uniqueness of referring to "her seed." This usage is an *hapax*. No other use of *zera'* (seed) in the Hebrew Bible has a feminine third singular possessive suffix. *Zera'* does appear many times in the Old Testament with the entire possibility of variety of masculine possessive suffixes. This being true, and in the light of Paul's speaking of one "born of woman" (Gal. 4:4), it appears most reasonable to the English reader to argue, "We ordinarily do not speak of 'seed of the woman.' We speak of 'seed of the man.' 'Seed of the woman' [a phrase which does not actually occur in the Bible but which has been coined to express the argument] can only be one virgin-born. There is no instance of one with only a female parent other than that of Jesus, born of Mary." Hence it is argued that we have here a clear and convincing prediction of the Virgin Birth.

Unknown to the English reader is the fact that *zera'* (seed) has the second person feminine possessive suffix in three cases in the Hebrew Bible. The reader's lack of knowledge is amply explained by the simple fact that variety has been used by the translators, and in these three cases the word at issue is rendered "descendants" and not "seed." *Zera'* is a collective noun and may be considered either as singular (Gen. 4:25; 21:13; 1 Sam. 1:11) or as plural. It is sometimes affirmed that it is not used in the Old Testament of a remote single descendant; but even should this prove true, we would have only the same question we have in Paul when he affirms that Abraham's seed means Christ (Gal. 3:16), and then before the end of the chapter says that all believing persons are heirs of the promise. They are Abraham's children.

Zera' with a feminine possessive suffix is used to describe the descendants of Hagar (Gen. 16:10) and the descendants of Rebecca (Gen. 24:60). Their immediate children are not under consideration; a virgin birth is not in view. Abraham is the father of Hagar's son, and they are jointly ancestors of her descendants. Isaac is to be the father of Rebecca's children. She is not yet married when the blessing in which the relevant statement is made is expressed. No one would care to argue either that these children or their posterity were virgin-born or that they in any way prefigure a virgin birth. There is a third case in which *zera'* with a feminine possessive suffix occurs. In it, plants in Adonis gardens grow from seed planted by Israel (Is. 17:11). Israel is, of course, a feminine noun in Hebrew, but in this case is not really relevant to the question we are discussing.

The only grammatical difference between the cases of Hagar and Rebecca and that of Eve is that in the one case the third feminine is used while in the other two the second person feminine is used. The use in Gen. 3:15 would not exclude a virgin birth, but judged from the grammatical viewpoint, the "woman's seed" argument is a broken reed of a staff that will not stand investigation.

This question is a different question from that of whether or not Gen. 3:15 has messianic import. Early Christian apologists thought that it did; the *Targum of Ps. Jonathan,* which is post-Christian in date, applies it to the days of the Messiah. Actually Gen. 3:15 is echoed in the New Testament once, but not in a virgin birth setting. Paul uses its wording to describe the victory over Satan, appealing not to "her seed," but to the other member of the Genesis phrase: "He shall bruise your head." Paul makes God the subject: "Then the God of peace will soon crush Satan under your feet" (Rom. 16:20).

The ignoring of this phenomenon can hardly be laid

upon the translation tradition. The Septuagint used *sperma* in each of these three passages; the Latin used *semen* in each of them. And shocking enough to learn, the English translations from the time of William Tyndale have all used "seed" (with spelling variations) in all three of the passages until one comes to the RSV. Had the Greek, Latin, or English reader merely checked his concordance he could have seen that his basic assumption—that using "seed" with a feminine possessive was unique to Gen. 3:15—was erroneous.

One finds "his seed" as a category in *Cruden's Concordance*, but though "her seed" is in the KJV, it is not listed as a category in that tool. There is one further passage (this one in the New Testament) which has a feminine possessive with "seed." It is Rev. 12:17. The dragon makes war "with the rest of her offspring" (*loipōn tou spermatos autēs*; Vulgate: *reliquis de semine eius*). No thinking person could suppose this verse has anything to do with the Virgin Birth. "The rest of her offspring" are believing people.

4

"When a Man . . ."

Deuteronomy 24:1-4

FORM

The regulation of Deut. 24:1-4 is stated in the form of a law which is known as casuistic or hypothetical law—the sort which Ex. 21:1 heads by the term *mishpatim*—"ordinances." Such regulations in Hebrew are introduced with the particles *ki* (when or supposed that . . . ; Deut. 22:13) or *'im* (if).[1] The persons concerned are

[1]Friedrich H. W. Gesenius, *Gesenius' Hebrew Grammar*, ed. Emil Kautzsch, 2d English ed., revised by Arthur E. Cowley (Oxford, England: Clarendon Press, 1910), 122 gg, hh. Hereafter cited as *GKC*.

spoken of in the third person. The law invariably has the protasis and the apodosis of a conditional sentence.[2] The form is very prevalent in the laws of Exodus 21ff. and is paralleled in the law codes of the Middle East—codes of Lipit-Ishtar, Eshnunna, Ur-Nammu, Hammurabi, the Hittites, and the Middle Assyrians. In this form of law, a hypothetical situation which is likely to be encountered in society is described, often with detailed conditions specified, and then the law governing that situation is announced.

WHERE DOES THE LEGAL ENACTMENT BEGIN?

A major question to be solved in the exegesis of Deut. 24:1-4 is simply that of determining where the hypothetical case is being described and where the legal pronouncement begins. The English translations contribute to this perplexity. The KJV and ASV following the Latin Vulgate give a jussive force to the first three verses, considering that the condition is stated in verse 1a, and that verse 1b—the giving of the bill of divorce—is a demand of the law.[3] Hence, these versions are liable to the interpretation that divorce and the writ of divorce were being provided for. Furthermore, in this passage, in these versions, the woman seems given permission to marry a second man (v. 2); and finally, a third regulation prohibits her remarriage to her first husband. The RSV and other modern translations more correctly consider

[2]A. Alt, "The Origins of Israelite Law," in *Essays on Old Testament History and Religion*, trans. R. A. Wilson (Garden City, N.Y.: Doubleday, 1968), pp. 112ff.

[3]R. C. Campbell, "Teachings of the Old Testament Concerning Divorce," *Foundations* 6 (1963):174-78.

that the hypothetical situation contains a series of conditions and that the legally binding pronouncement comes only at verse 4.

In Hebrew the section begins the protasis, and then the subsidiary conditions are all added on with the repeated use of the conjunction *waw* (and). There are cases in Hebrew of the conditional sentence where the apodosis is introduced with *waw* followed by the perfect tense of the verb,[4] as the KJV scholars seem to have taken verse 1; but having taken the *waw* as introducing the apodosis, those translators were left without a particle with which to introduce their second conditional sentence and had to supply "if" twice in verse 3. There is no logical reason why *waw* should be taken in verse 1b as introducing the apodosis. It is more normal to take all the *waws* of the passage (vv. 1-3) as coordinate, setting up the situation that is to be regulated.

The law of Deut. 24:1-4 is not a law instituting divorce, nor is it prescribing the bill of divorce—Jesus' questioners notwithstanding (Mt. 19:7; Mk. 10:4).[5] There is no permission given for the woman to form a second marriage. The divorce, the bill of divorce, and the second marriage are only parts of the description of the situation which had developed. The legal enactment is that the first husband cannot take back the woman when these specified conditions exist. The protasis has multiple conditions stated. One may see in Ex. 21:1-6 another such lengthy protasis in the same sort of style, dealing with

[4]*GKC*, 112 kk; 159 g.

[5]Matthew uses the word "command" (*entellesthai*) for their question (v. 7) but *epitrepein* (allowed) for the answer of Jesus (v. 8). Mark uses *entellesthai* for Jesus' question to them (v. 3) and has the Pharisee say that Moses "allowed" (*epitrepein*). Then Mark uses *entolē* (which may be used for all legal regulations) for Jesus' characterization of Moses' statement.

the Hebrew slave who does not want his freedom. Yet another law of multiple conditions dealing with flogging is found in Deut. 25:1-3.

In the situation described in Deut. 24:1-4, there are three conditions to be fulfilled before the law is applicable. First, the woman is divorced and is furnished with proper papers to establish the divorce. Second, the woman is remarried; that she can do so is assumed. Third, the second husband either divorces her or he dies. It would appear that, according to custom, she is legally free to contract a third marriage. But the specific law here announced prohibits her first husband from remarrying her; reunion with him is forbidden. The law is without parallel in the ancient world. Later Roman law permitted a man to remarry his first wife after she had remarried and had divorced her second husband.[6] Muslim law prefers remarriage with the former husband in such cases.[7]

THE ORIGIN OF DIVORCE

Though the origin of marriage and its ideal are described in the creation story (Genesis 2), the origin of divorce, its rightness and wrongness, and the question of remarriage of the divorced are not directly discussed in the Pentateuch. In the post-exilic period, the prophet Malachi states for the Lord, "I hate divorce" (Mal. 2:16); but the Pentateuch has no such direct statement.

No Hebrew law institutes divorce any more than it does polygamy and concubinage. The custom, which

[6]Boaz Cohen, "Concerning Divorce in Roman Law," *The American Academy of Jewish Research Proceedings* 21 (1952):9.

[7]Qur'an *Sura* 2:229ff.

must be almost as old as the race itself, was recognized in Israel and is assumed everywhere.[8] The husband seems to have had unlimited right to divorce his wife. Abraham dismissed Hagar (Gen. 21:14). There are cases of forced divorce in the Old Testament, such as those at the time of the return from exile (Ezra 10:3, 19; Neh. 13:1-3, 23ff.); however, the future marital status of those putting away their wives and that of the wives themselves is not discussed.

In the Pentateuch the priest and the high priest could not marry a divorced woman (Lev. 21:7, 14); other men likely did. Men forfeited the right of divorce for certain acts of misconduct. The man who falsely accused his bride of premarital unchastity could never divorce her (Deut. 22:13-21),[9] and the man who seduced a girl was required to marry her with no possibility for later divorce (Deut. 22:28-29).[10] These laws restricted the husband's unlimited right to divorce his wife. The divorced woman was called *gerushah* (one driven out; Lev. 21:14; Num. 30:10; Ezek. 44:22). The divorced daughter of a priest who was without children could eat of her father's food (Lev. 22:13) just as she could have done had she been widowed. The divorced woman's vow was binding upon her, whereas the married woman's vow could be negated by her husband (Num. 30:6-9). Figuratively, the Lord is said to have divorced Israel

[8]Evidence for the prevalence of divorce in the ancient Middle East is summarized in Jack P. Lewis, "From the Beginning It Was Not So," in *Your Marriage Can Be Great*, ed. T. B. Warren (Jonesboro, Ark.: National Christian Press, 1978), pp. 412-13.

[9]By the first century A.D. the woman had the option of whether or not she would remain in such a marriage (Philo *The Special Laws* 3.82). The law was also modified to free the man from living with a demonstrated adulteress (Josephus *Antiquities* 4.3; cf. Mishnah *Ketuboth* 3:4-5).

[10]See Mishnah *Ketuboth* 3:5.

at the exile (Jer. 3:8). The second marriage for the divorcee is nowhere specifically sanctioned in the Old Testament, but Deut. 24:1-4 assumes that such marriages take place.

The law does not envision the possibility of a woman's divorcing her husband. It likely was not done in early Israel.[11] The slave girl taken as a wife could gain her freedom if her master did not furnish her with food, clothing, and sexual needs (Ex. 21:10-11). The details of how she established her case are not given. She likely would have to establish her claim before proper authorities; but it is her husband who grants her her freedom. Josephus informs us that when Salome divorced her husband, Costobarus,[12] and when Herodias divorced Herod Philip,[13] their acts were contrary to the custom of the Jews. Later Judaism did grant the woman right of divorce where the husband was a leper, was afflicted with polypus (some offensive catarrhal affliction), or was engaged in a repulsive trade like collecting dog excrements, smelting copper, or tanning hides. It was a debated question whether the woman could change her mind about the marriage if she knew of the occupation of her husband before marriage.[14] Later also, divorce was granted for inability or failure to perform conjugal duties, for depriving the wife of her liberty to work, for cruel and inhuman treatment, and for non-support.[15]

[11]The woman of Elephantine could initiate divorce proceedings; see Y. Muff, *Studies in Aramaic Legal Papyri from Elephantine*, Studia et Documenta VIII (New York: KTAV, 1973), p. 55.

[12]Josephus *Antiquities* 15.7.10 (259).

[13]Ibid., 18.5.4 (136).

[14]Mishnah *Ketuboth* 7:10.

[15]Mishnah *Nedarim* 11:12; *Ketuboth* 5:5-6; 7:2-7; *T.B. Ketuboth* 77a.

THE CONDITIONS OF THE LAW

She Does Not Find Favor in His Eyes

The expression "to find favor in one's eyes" (Gen. 6:8; 18:2; 19:19; etc.) occurs at least forty-five times in the Old Testament (ASV) for pleasing God or man in various ways. It occurs in the negative—"to not find favor"—only twice (Deut. 24:1; Num. 11:11) and is used for the male-female attraction only here in Deut. 24:1, though some element of that attraction is possibly in the background in three occurrences in Esther's appeal to King Ahasuerus (Esther 5:8; 7:3; 8:5). The expression within itself casts no light on the details of the wife's lack of attraction for her husband that could contribute to the situation the law describes.

That divorce, for no other cause than that the wife did not please the husband, was tolerated may perhaps be inferred from Ex. 21:7-11, where the Hebrew slave girl who does not please her master is not set free as male slaves are. But she may be redeemed, and if the master does not furnish her her conjugal rights (food, clothing, and sex), she goes free without payment.

She Has Some Unclean Thing in Her

The puzzling phrase "some indecency" (*'ervath dabhar*—literally, "nakedness of a thing"; LXX: *aschēmon pragma*; Vulgate: *aliquam foeditatem*)[16] occurs twice in the Old Testament (Deut. 23:14; 24:1); but the other occurrence, dealing with sanitation rather than a moral offense, does not furnish a clear definition for the

[16]David Daube, "Repudium in Deuteronomy," in *Neotestamentica et Semetica*, ed. E. E. Ellis and Max Wilcox (Edinburgh, Scotland: T. & T. Clark, 1969), pp. 236-40.

term under consideration. Onkelos in the Targum gave *'averath pitgam* (the transgression of a thing), but *'ervath* does not come from the root *'abhar*—"to transgress." *'Ervath* (from *'arah*—"to be naked") elsewhere describes shameful exposure of the body (Gen. 9:22; Ex. 20:26; Is. 20:4; 47:3; Lam. 1:8; Ezek. 16:8, 36-37; 23:29; Hos. 2:11 [9]), illicit and abnormal sexual practices (Leviticus 18; 20), and exposure of human excrement (Deut. 23:14). In this last case it describes what is unbecoming, not what is immoral.

Should we assume that the term suggests that the husband finds his bride has been unchaste before marriage, we are reminded that death was the punishment for the woman for premarital unchastity (Deut. 22:21). Should we assume that adultery after marriage is spoken of, that crime also carried a death penalty (Gen. 38:24; Lev. 20:10; Num. 5:11ff.; Deut. 22:22ff.; cf. Ezek. 16:40; 23:47; Jn. 8:15).[17] Bestiality (Ex. 22:19; Lev. 18:23; 20:16; Deut. 27:21) and incest (Lev. 20:11-12, 14, 17) carried a death penalty. For men, homosexuality (or sodomy) carried a death penalty (Lev. 18:22; 20:13). Female perversion in this area is not specifically discussed in the Old Testament. Being childless was no doubt a particularly serious handicap for a wife (Gen. 16:1; 1 Sam. 1:5-7). Rabbinic rule recognized ten years of childless marriage as a basis for divorce;[18] Philo recommended divorce in such cases, but was willing to pardon those who out of affection continued in marriage;[19] but there is no convincing reason to link *'ervath dabhar* with this condition. The term *'ervath dabhar* would seem to

[17]See J. J. Rabinowitz, "The 'Great Sin' in Ancient Egyptian Marriage Contracts," *JNES* 18 (1959):73; W. L. Moran, "The Scandal of the 'Great Sin' at Ugarit," *JNES* 18 (1959):280-81.

[18]*T.B. Yebamoth* 64a; *Ketuboth* 77a.

[19]Philo *The Special Laws* 3.34-35.

describe anything, other than the punishable acts mentioned above, which the man finds distasteful in his bride.

The lack of specificity in *'ervath dabhar* set the stage for the later discussion of the schools of Shammai and Hillel who assumed that Moses was laying down the basis on which a divorce could be granted. The Shammaites considered that *'ervath* must imply some sort of lewd behavior on the part of the woman;[20] however, in the sources extant they are not specific about just what sort of behavior must be involved. According to them, the divorce is granted for causes of immorality. The Hillelites put emphasis upon *dabhar* and took *'ervath*, not in the sense of "lewdness," but in the sense of a "defect." They then said if she "burned his bread," he could divorce her. Some scholars have assumed that "burned his bread" is a euphemism for behavior other than defective cooking. Be that as it may, the attitude justified easy divorce. Rabbi Akiba later moved past both these words and centered attention on the phrase "if she find no favor in his eyes," concluding that if one found a more attractive woman, he could divorce his wife.[21] Philo of Alexandria (10 B.C.-A.D. 60) also spoke of divorce given "under any pretense whatever";[22] and Josephus, who had himself divorced his wife bcause he was "displeased at her conduct,"[23] said, "He who desires to be divorced from his wife for any cause whatsoever and many such causes happen among men, let him in writing give assurance that he no longer wishes to live with her as his wife."[24] Despite these laxities, the general rabbinic attitude,

[20]Mishnah *Gittin* 9:10.
[21]Ibid.
[22]Philo *The Special Laws* 3.30-31.
[23]Josephus *Life* 76 (426); cf. 75 (414-15).
[24]Josephus *Antiquities* 4.8.23 (253).

while recognizing the right of divorce by mutual consent, decried divorce of the wife by the husband.[25] Interesting as these later developments are, they should not be read back into the original law. We are without clear definition of *'ervath dabhar*.

He Gives Her a Bill of Divorce

It has been thought that divorces in Assyria and then much later (fifth century B.C.) in Elephantine required only an oral declaration.[26] The bill of divorce in Roman law has been thought to have been introduced only as late as the time of Diocletian (A.D. 284-305).[27] We are without details as to the first origin of the custom, but the bill of divorce (*sepher kerithuth*; LXX: *biblion tou apostasiou*; Vulgate: *libellum repudii*), later called the *get*, is likely of great antiquity and is not an innovation of Deuteronomy. It is here mentioned as a part of the protasis and not as a part of the apodosis—the enactment of the law. Its object was to make the divorce final and to prevent the husband from reasserting his rights over the wife or of accusing her of adultery should she form another marriage (cf. Is. 50:1; Jer. 3:8; Mt. 5:31; 19:7; Mk. 10:4). It was very important in a society in which intercourse with a married woman could lead to capital punishment for adultery.

The one actual divorce paper we have from the Tannaitic period is that dating about A.D. 111 which comes from the caves at Murabba'at in which Joseph, son

[25]D. W. Amram, *The Jewish Law of Divorce According to Bible and Talmud*, 2d ed. (New York: Hermon Press, 1968), pp. 38-39.

[26]R. de Vaux, *Ancient Israel*, trans. John McHugh (New York: McGraw-Hill, 1961), p. 35; Reuven Yaron, *Introduction to the Law of the Aramaic Papyri* (Oxford, England: Clarendon Press, 1961), p. 54.

[27]Amram, *Jewish Law of Divorce*, pp. 139-40.

of Naqsan, divorces Miriam, daughter of Yonatan, who resides at Masada. He declares, "I divorce and repudiate of my own free will, you . . . who was my wife formerly, in such a way that you are free to go and become wife of any Jewish man that you wish." He attests that the bill is his letter of divorce; it is given to her and it is signed by Joseph himself, by the scribe, and by two witnesses.[28] In the Mishnah, like wording is used for the bill of divorce. Rabbi Yehudah gave the form, "You have herewith from me a bill of dismissal, a document of release and a letter of freedom, that you may go and be married to any man you like." Later sources also used the phrases, "You are sent away" or "You are divorced."[29]

He Sends Her Out of the House

In the Code of Hammurabi a woman could sue for divorce and if she won was allowed to take her marriage portion and return to her father's house (law 142); but if it was proved that she had been a bad wife, she was thrown into the water (law 143). No provision is made in the Old Testament for the wife to divorce her husband. The phrase "sends her out of his house" (v. 4) uses the *pi'el* form of *shalach*, which is the customary term for divorce (Deut. 22:19, 29; Is. 50:1).

She Marries Another Man

The rightness or wrongness of a second marriage is not

[28]J. T. Milik, "Acte de Répudation, en Arameen," in *Discoveries in the Judean Desert II, Les Grottes de Murabba'at,* ed. P. Benoit, J. T. Milik, and R. de Vaux (Oxford, England: Clarendon Press, 1961), pp. 104ff.

[29]Mishnah *Gittin* 9:3; *T.B. Qiddushin* 5b; see Z. W. Falk, *Introduction to Jewish Law of the Second Commonwealth* (Leiden, The Netherlands: E. J. Brill, 1972), pp. 138-42.

the point under discussion in this law. In a world in which woman's function and occupation was marriage, it is assumed likely that another marriage would be formed. We do not know whether or not there were people unmarried by choice in Hebrew society. Jeremiah seems in a unique category when the Lord commanded him not to marry and not to beget children (Jer. 16:2). Later rabbinic regulations shamed the unmarried man. R. Eleazar said, "Any man who has no wife is no proper man; for it is said, 'Male and female created he them and called their name Adam' "[30]—that is, only when the male and female were united were they called Adam (man). R. Eleazar made failure to propagate the race equivalent to shedding blood.[31]

The Second Man Hates Her

Sane' (hate) is used frequently in the Old Testament for a man's attitude toward a woman. Used also in Hammurabi's Code (law 142) for the woman's hating her husband, it is not necessarily a violent aversion, but is simply the antithesis to love. It describes Jacob's attitude to Leah compared with that to Rachel (Gen. 29:31, 33). A man may have a loved wife and a hated one (Deut. 21:15-17). It describes the attitude of the man who slanders his wife's premarital conduct (Deut. 22:13, 16). Samson's wife and her father accused him of hating her (Judg. 14:16; 15:2). Ammon hated Tamar after he had ravished her (2 Sam. 13:15). The hated (unloved) woman may get a husband (Prov. 30:23). Israel in her exile is described as a hated one (Is. 60:15).[32] In this law of Deuteronomy,

[30]*T.B. Yebamoth* 63a.

[31]Ibid., 63b.

[32]Reuven Yaron, "On Divorce in Old Testament Times," *Revue Internationale des Droits de l'Antiquite*, ser. 3, vol. 4 (1957):117-28.

then, the point in this detail is that the second man does not want the woman to continue as his wife. The particular cause is not important.

The Second Husband Divorces Her or Dies

The hypothetical situation again assumes the possibility of divorce, with due papers being given to establish it, theoretically making the woman free for marriage again.

Death also dissolved a marriage. David was free to take Abigail when Nabal was dead (1 Sam. 25:39-40) and Bathsheba when Uriah was dead (2 Sam. 11:27). David is not condemned for marrying a widow, but for his sin with her while her husband was yet alive. ". . . a married woman is bound by law to her husband as long as he lives; but if her husband dies she is discharged from the law concerning the husband" (Rom. 7:2).

The various stipulations in Deuteronomy which we have surveyed have as their point the making clear that according to custom the woman was now available for marriage.

Complications in administering the law like those raised by later rabbis when they considered the status of the woman who, thinking her husband was dead, erroneously had entered a second marriage and then later had found that her husband was still living[33] are not considered in the Pentateuch. Conditions of war in many periods of history have left women without knowledge whether their missing husbands are dead or alive. In the Code of Hammurabi, the woman deserted by her hus-

[33]See Reuven Yaron, "Mistake-Occasioned Polygamy," in *Studies in Jewish Legal History, Essays in Honour of David Daube*, ed. Bernard S. Jackson (London: Jewish Chronicle Publications, 1974), pp. 203-26.

band without support (law 134) enters another man's house and is free of blame. Should the first husband later return, she must go back to her bridegroom; but the children she has borne to the second man remain with him (law 135). However, the returning husband who "hated his city and fled" cannot seize his wife; she can remain with the second man because her husband's act is considered blameworthy (law 136).

THE ENACTMENT

The apodosis of the law of Deuteronomy, taking the form of an absolute, permanent prohibition, using the negative *lo'* with the imperfect of the verb—*lo' yukhal*—carries the strongest expectation of obedience.[34] The form is used especially in enforcing divine commands—for example, those using the second person pronoun in the Ten Commandments (Ex. 20:3-5, 7, 10). However, the negative command with the third person (as here) is also possible (cf. Prov. 16:10). The prohibition announced is: He shall not take her back!

The passage grammatically displays anacoluthon[35] in that having started in the third person, there is then in verse 4 a shift to second person—"You make the land to sin." This shift does not soften the prohibition.

In considering Israel's relation with God, Jeremiah raises a parallel question (Jer. 3:1).[36] Will a man take back a woman who has been divorced and has become another man's wife? Would not that greatly pollute the

[34]*GKC* 107 o.

[35]Ibid., 167 b.

[36]J. D. Martin, "The Forensic Background to Jeremiah III.1," *Vetus Testamentum* 19 (January 1969):82-92.

land? The prophet's answer is that though man may not do so, the Lord can do it with his bride Israel who has played the harlot with many lovers.

An apparent difficulty in the interpretation we have given arises from the Gospel statement, "It was also said, 'Whoever divorces his wife, let him give her a certificate of divorce'" (Mt. 5:31). Many have understood the phrase "it was also said" to be implying that "Moses said"—that is, that the law demanded the giving of the certificate of divorce. However, in this passage Jesus is not giving a direct quotation from either the Hebrew or Greek Bible. We have already considered the structure of the Hebrew passage and have seen that the giving of the written divorce is mentioned only as a secondary condition of the situation. The imperative *dotō autē apostasion* (Let him give her a bill of divorce) of the Gospel may be compared with the Septuagint of Deut. 24:1ff.: *kai grapsei autē biblion apostasiou* . . . (and shall write her a bill of divorce). Here the future indicative is functioning as a subjunctive. The Septuagint, like the Hebrew, considers that the sentence is a conditional one of numerous conditions creating the situation, and the enactment is reached only in the declaration at verse 4—the first husband cannot marry her again. It seems clear that the equation of "it was also said" to "Moses said"—making an imperative out of a secondary condition of the situation—is not a safe conclusion to draw. Later in the series in the Gospel of Matthew, the statement, "You have heard that it was said, 'You shall love your neighbor and hate your enemy'" (Mt. 5:43) is also not a statement from the law of Moses.

THE PURPOSE OF THE ENACTMENT

Some[37] have felt the law of Deuteronomy was designed to protect the first marriage by reminding the husband that should he hastily divorce, he might not get the woman back even if he wanted her.[38] But this can hardly be the purpose of the law. Psychologically, one is not going to be concerned about getting back a woman that he wants to divorce. Furthermore, the law puts no impediment in the way of remarriage if a marriage has not in the meantime been contracted by the woman with a second husband.[39]

Others have thought the law was designed to protect the second marriage.[40]

Had the husband divorced the wife in a fit of anger and she married another, they cannot rekindle the old flame. While it is true that in practice the law would not encourage the woman who was wanting to return to her first husband to act so that her second husband would be disgusted with her and would divorce her, and though neither would it encourage the first husband and the woman to plot the death of the second husband that she might be free,[41] there must be other reasons back of this

[37]W. G. Jordan, *Commentary on the Book of Deuteronomy* (New York: Macmillan Co., 1911), p. 172. See the discussion of Reuven Yaron, "The Restoration of Marriage," *Journal of Jewish Studies* 17 (1966):1-11.

[38]A man's wife being taken forcibly from him and given to another is the last and most bitter degradation which can be imposed upon him (Deut. 28:30; 2 Sam. 12:11; 1 Kings 20:3; Jer. 6:12; 8:10; cf. Amos 7:17).

[39]See Mishnah *Eduyoth* 4:7; *Sotah* 8:3.

[40]J. Morgenstern, "The Book of the Covenant, Part II," *Hebrew Union College Annual* 7 (1930):157n.

[41]The Code of Hammurabi (law 153) prescribes impaling for the wife guilty of this act.

law which put a check on wife swapping.

Three reasons are given why the husband cannot take the wife again. First, she is defiled as far as her first husband is concerned. Under the law, sex relations with one to whom one is not entitled—such as a neighbor's wife—defiles (Lev. 18:20), and the woman with whom such relations are had is defiled (Num. 5:13, 20). The passive *hothpa'el* form is found in only a few cases in the Old Testament (Lev. 13:55-56; Is. 34:6).[42] For the root *tame'* the *hothpa'el* occurs only here—*huṭṭamma'ah.* The *pi'el* and *niph'al* of *tame'* mean "make unclean" or "make oneself unclean" (Lev. 11:43; Num. 5:3). The phrase passes into Greek as *meta to mianthēnai autēn* and then into Latin as *polluta est.*[43] That is, the law has theological implications in addition to its strict legal ones. Some have thought that the implication of the prohibition is that her act is equal to adultery and that the law anticipates Jesus' declaration, ". . . whoever marries a divorced woman commits adultery" (Mt. 5:32);[44] however, this attitude overlooks the fact that no condemnation is specifically given of her marriage to husband number two; nor is it said that she is forbidden to number three—so long as he is not number one.

Second, for him to take her back is an abomination (*to'ebhah*) in the sight of the Lord. *To'ebhah* from the root *ta'abh* (to be abhorred) occurs 116 times as a noun and twenty-three times as a verb in the Old Testament. It is sixteen times in Deuteronomy and earlier was four times

[42]*GKC* 54 h.

[43]Philo *The Special Laws* 3.30-31, says he stamps on his character two of the greatest iniquities, adultery and pandering.

[44]S. R. Driver, *A Critical and Exegetical Commentary on Deuteronomy,* International Critical Commentary, 3d ed. (Edinburgh, Scotland: T. & T. Clark, 1902), p. 272.

in the proverbs of Amenemope.[45] The occurrences cover a variety of acts ranging from food prohibitions (Deut. 14:3), idolatrous practices (Deut. 7:25; 12:31; 13:14), magic (Deut. 18:12), sex offences (Lev. 18:22ff.), and transvestite clothing (Deut. 22:5) to ethical wrongs (Deut. 25:14-16; Prov. 6:16-19). Common to all these usages is the notion of irregularity. The act offends the accepted order, ritual, or morals. The law of Deuteronomy 24 declares, then, that God is offended should the prohibited act take place.

Third, by the act, one makes the land which the Lord gives you to sin. The *hiph'il* of *chata'* occurs most frequently in the Old Testament in connection with an Israelite king, like Jeroboam, who is said to have sinned and to have made Israel to sin (1 Kings 14:16; 15:26, 30, 34; 16:26; 22:52), but is also used of Manasseh and Judah (2 Kings 21:11). The second person *hiph'il* occurs here in verse 4 and in oracles against Baasha (1 Kings 16:2) and Ahab (1 Kings 21:22). The land is being personified and, hence, can be spoken of as sinning.

That God has given Israel the land (cf. Deut. 4:21) is a frequently encountered idea in the Old Testament, and the idea that unchastity defiles the land is frequently stated (Lev. 18:25, 28; 19:29; Jer. 3:2, 9; Hos. 4:3). Murder (Num. 35:33f.), leaving the executed man hanging (Deut. 21:23), idolatry (Ps. 106:38), and contact with corpses (Num. 5:3; 19:13) also pollute the land. Like Deuteronomy, Jeremiah considers that marital perversity "pollutes" (Jeremiah uses *chanaph* instead of *tame'*) the land (Jer. 3:2).

[45]See Moshe Weinfeld, *Deuteronomy and the Deuteronomic School* (Oxford, England: Clarendon Press, 1972), p. 268.

THE LAW IGNORED?

It has often been asked if the case of Michal and David is not a transgression of Pentateuchal law. Michal loved David, and he betrothed her to himself at the price of a hundred Philistine foreskins (1 Sam. 18:20-23; 2 Sam. 3:14); but after she helped him escape from her father, Saul (1 Sam. 19:11ff.), Saul gave her to Paltiel (1 Sam. 25:44). When David became king, he demanded that Ishbosheth restore Michal to him. When she was taken from her husband, Paltiel, he followed her weeping until he was driven off by Abner (2 Sam. 3:15-16). Some writers have attempted to apologize for what seemed to them to be a transgression of the law by contending that David's marriage with Michal had not been consummated when she was taken from him; others suggest that her marriage with Paltiel had not been consummated; but neither of these two cases is convincing. The conditions specified in Deuteronomy are not present in this case; hence, the law is not applicable and is not flaunted. David had not divorced her; she had not been rejected by the second man, nor had he died. She had been given to another man, but she was still David's wife and he claimed her.[46]

The same is true with the wife of Hosea (assuming that the woman of chapter 1 of the book is the same woman as that of chapter 3). Her husband could overlook her waywardness and take her back. Isaiah (50:1) then can insist that in the case of God and Israel, there has been no divorce; hence, there is no impediment that would prevent God from taking wayward Israel back to himself.

[46]The rabbis permitted remarriage after a divorce followed by illicit relations with another man, Mishnah *Sotah* 2:6.

Biblical law did not demand that the wayward woman be divorced. In Babylonian law (law 129), the husband decided whether to drown the woman along with her lover caught in the act of adultery or to spare her. If he wished to spare her, the king could also spare the man. Later rabbinic law required that the adulterous woman be divorced and that a remarriage of a man to a wife married to another in the meantime must be terminated.[47]

CONCLUSION

Detailed exegesis of Deut. 24:1-4 suggests that the rabbis were on a wrong track when they conceived the passage to be stating the basis on which a divorce could be given. It also suggests that modern commentators are engaging in homiletics, not in exegesis, when they deduce lessons about divorce which were not the intent of the lawgiver. Rather than teaching about conditions of divorce, the passage is prohibiting remarriage with a divorced woman who has meanwhile been married to another.

It is little wonder that Jesus, without disputing in detail the presuppositions of his audience, moved back to the original ideal for marriage announced in Genesis 2 (Mt. 19:8), and that Paul said, ". . . the wife should not separate from her husband (but if she does, let her remain single or else be reconciled to her husband)—and that the husband should not divorce his wife" (1 Cor. 7:10-11; cf. Rom. 7:2).

[47]Mishnah *Yebamoth* 4:2, 12; *T.B. Sotah* 27b-28a; *Yebamoth* 11a-b; 49b. See Louis Epstein, *Marriage Laws in the Bible and the Talmud* (Cambridge: Harvard University Press, 1942), p. 295.

5

Difficult Texts From The Psalms and Proverbs

OVERVIEWING, ANALYZING, AND INTERPRETING THE PSALMS

The book of Psalms is a miscellaneous anthology of religious lyric poetry. Its 150 poems were composed over an undefined number of centuries by many writers. The headings, which are not thought to be of equal age with the poems themselves, attribute some Psalms to Moses, David, Solomon, Jeduthun, Heman, Asaph, Etham the Ezrahite, and to the sons of Korah. The Psalms are divided into five sections (1-41, 42-72, 73-89, 90-106, 107-150) each of which comes to an end with a doxology. The collection had already been made before our earliest knowledge about the Psalms. History has not preserved any information telling us who is responsible for gathering the Psalms together, about the circumstances in which it was done, or about the guiding principles followed.

The nature of Hebrew poetry was first discovered by Robert Lowth about 1753. Its essence is not rhymed syllables as is true of English poetry; but it has a poetic line, usually of two parts, in which there is a balance of stressed ideas. These stresses may be two, three, or four; however, the dirge or elegiac meter has three stresses in the first half of the line followed by two in the last half. In addition, there is the phenomenon called parallelism in which ideas are repeated with only slight variation. The parallel may be synonymous: "Moreover by them is thy servant warned; in keeping them there is great reward" (Ps. 19:11). It may be antithetic: "A wise son makes a glad father, but a foolish son is a sorrow to his mother" (Prov. 10:1). Or, it may have several other possible forms.

In the classification of the Psalms, modern Psalms study classifies the Psalms in a number of literary types according to their content—the communal lament, the communal song of thanksgiving, the individual lament, the individual song of thanksgiving, the enthronement Psalms, the messianic Psalms, and yet others. Great emphasis is placed on trying to reconstruct the worship setting in Israel into which such compositions would fit. The Psalms must be dealt with in keeping with the intent of the writers in as far as that intent can be determined. Allowance must be made for what is called "poetic license." One does not read a poem in the factual way he reads a newspaper article if he wants to obtain the full benefit of the poem.

PSALMS 18, 35, 69, 109, 137: EXPLAINING THE IMPRECATORY PSALMS

The Bible depicts the whole gamut of human actions and emotions. Some actions depicted—like the attachment of Ruth and Naomi—are admirable; others—like the suicide of Ahithophel—are not. The actions of the men of Sodom are depicted in the same Testament that tells of the Shunammite woman who cared for Elisha. Some speakers in the Bible speak truth; others, such as the Assyrian commander, the old prophet, and the devil himself, do not speak truth. It is a part of the exegetical task to separate that which is admirable from that which is not, and that which is truthful from that which is not.

Unlike those parts of the Bible where God speaks directly to man, the Psalms are to a large extent man's pouring out his emotions to God. They have sometimes been described as a combination of the hymn book and the prayer book of the Israelites. With complete frankness, the lyric poetry lays bare the human soul. That soul does not at all times measure up to the highest ideals announced in the Old Testament, not to mention its falling short of the ideals of the further revelation of man's duty made known in Christ Jesus. A discrimination must be exercised in determining that which is to be followed and that which may be of value chiefly to illustrate attitudes and emotions to be avoided. The Shepherd Psalm (Psalm 23) will speak to men's souls as long as they tend to wander like sheep and to find in the Lord their Good Shepherd. The imprecation on the Edomites (Psalm 137), though accurately describing the feelings that naturally well up in the hearts of those greatly abused, fits less well into the emotions one can allow himself to indulge in. Especially is this true if he takes seriously the admonitions: ". . . never avenge yourselves . . . but leave it to the wrath of God; . . ." (Rom. 12:19), and ". . . pray for those who persecute you, . . ." (Mt. 5:44). The issue of the imprecatory Psalm is easily stated: How can it be right to pray for the destruction and doom of persons as is done in certain Psalms? Can the Christian use them?

"Imprecatory Psalms" are those that involve judgment, calamity, or curse on certain persons.[1] There are no Psalms that are entirely imprecatory, but eighteen (some count twenty-eight) have imprecatory elements, and thirteen of these are in their headings ascribed to David. These eighteen total 386 verses out of which only sixty-five have imprecation. Three Psalms (35, 69, 109) have a total of ninety-three verses, but out of them only twenty-three are imprecation. The strongest statements are seen in seven Psalms (35, 55, 59, 69, 79, 109, 137). Five of these are ascribed in their headings to David, one (79) to Asaph, and one (137) has no heading.

Various approaches, perhaps some less objectionable than others, attempt to deal with this element of the Psalms.

Some scholars deny the inspiration of the material, making them to be vindicative expressions of sinful men. In making such a claim, men ignore that 2 Samuel 1-2 states that David as a psalmist was inspired by the Spirit. Though David could be tempted to take vengeance

[1]I have made use of the studies of: Chalmers Martin, "The Imprecations in the Psalms," *Princeton Theological Review* 1, 4 (1903):537-53; Johannes G. Vos, "The Ethical Problem of the Imprecatory Psalms," *Westminster Theological Journal* 4 (May 1942):123-38; Raymond F. Surburg, "The Interpretation of the Imprecatory Psalms," *Springfielder* 39 (December 1975):88-102; Joseph Blenkinsopp, "Can We Pray the Cursing Psalms?" in *A Sketchbook of Biblical Theology* (London: Burns & Oates, 1968), pp. 83-87.

on Nabal (1 Sam. 25:21ff.) until turned from it by Abigail, as vindicative expressions, these statements do not fit with the charity David showed Saul when he spared him (1 Sam. 24:1-15; 26:1-25), the charity extended to Abishai (2 Sam. 16:10-11), the lament over the deaths of Saul (2 Sam. 1:19ff.) and Abner (2 Sam. 3:33-34), the kindness he showed to the descendants of Saul (2 Sam. 9:3), and the sparing of Shemei (2 Sam. 19:16ff.). The imprecatory Psalms themselves show that David was not ignorant of the obligation to do good for evil (Ps. 35:12ff.; 109:4-5). Men who deny the inspiration of the Psalms immediately set themselves in opposition to Jesus who himself echoes Ps. 137:9 in describing the fate of Jerusalem, using the exact verb that occurs in the Greek text of the psalm: "Your enemies will . . . dash you to the ground, you and your children within you, . . ." (Lk. 19:44). He quoted Ps. 69:4: "They hated me without a cause; . . ." (Jn. 15:25). His disciples remembered Ps. 69:9: ". . . zeal for thy house has consumed me, . . ." when Jesus cleansed the temple (Jn. 2:17). The New Testament also explicitly quotes portions of Psalms 69 and 109 as having the Holy Spirit as author and as depicting the work of Judas (Acts 1:20). It has been suggested that Rom. 2:9-10 describes the judicial blindness (cf. Rom. 10:25; cf. 1:21; Eph. 4:18) of the Jewish nation following the resurrection in terms of Ps. 69:22-23. Rom. 15:3 enforces the duty of pleasing our neighbor by a quotation of Ps. 69:9. These New Testament interpretations make clear that the one who denies the inspiration of the material has fallen into a serious problem.

Yet another approach is to allege that these sentiments belong to a primitive stage of revelation which was superceded with the giving of the New Testament.

Dispensationalism[2] insists that they belong to the dispensation of law and cannot be applied to the dispensation of grace. Even after one has dealt with the fact that the dispensational system itself is arbitrary and unscriptural and that it vitiates a great deal of Scripture, making it unsuited for Christian devotional use, he is still faced with the fact it is the Old Testament which says, "Vengeance belongeth unto me; I will recompense saith the Lord" (KJV). Paul, in forbidding vengeance (Rom. 12:19ff.), does so by citing Deut. 32:35 and Prov. 25:21-22. The law of Moses forbids private vengeance and insists that one must not bear a grudge (Lev. 19:18) and that he must deal kindly with his enemies by returning their straying animals and by helping with a distressed animal (Ex. 23:4-5). Job protests in his oath of clearing that he has not rejoiced at the ruin of him who hated him; he has not asked for his life with a curse (Job 31:29-30). Those rejecting dispensationalism who magnify the ethical gulf between the Testaments need to remember these statements.

Others have contended that the psalmist was not desiring the doom of the wicked but was merely predicting it on the basis that "... whatever a man sows, that he will also reap" (Gal. 6:7). While some instances in these psalms may be prediction, this case cannot be maintained for the totality if one looks at the actual wording of the Psalms. God is specifically addressed in the form of prayer.

Yet another effort attempts to allegorize the statements and to make them prayers against spiritual enemies instead of against actual human beings. This arbitrary system is refuted by the wording that is aimed

[2]C. I. Scofield, ed., *The Scofield Reference Bible* (New York: Oxford University Press, 1945), p. 599.

at actual persons whether they are known or unknown to us.

Another effort would see these Psalms as cries of outraged humanity to the just God to judge and condemn the wicked—not just a cry for personal vengeance. But this case does not fit all the Psalms, and it does not deal with the imprecations involving helpless children: "Let there be none . . . to pity his fatherless children! . . ." (Ps. 109:12), and "Happy shall he be who takes your little ones and dashes them against the rock!" (Ps. 137:9).

Another effort would point out that man is a creature whose chief end is the glorification of God—not just the seeking of the welfare of man, without regard to what he has done, as humanism would insist it is. The Christian is not to pray for the man who has sinned unto death (1 Jn. 5:16). When the glory of God and the welfare of man clash, the glory of God takes precedence. The believer must seek the glory of God. God, as the Judge of the universe, is acting within the limits of right to destroy evil and evil men by whatever means he chooses: natural catastrophe, war, or judicial punishment. He has the unquestioned right to destroy evil in his universe. Some of the imprecations are not expressions of desire for personal vengeance, but are prayers for judicial vindication of the name of God: "Consume them in wrath, consume them till they are no more, that men may know that God rules over Jacob to the ends of the earth" (Ps. 59:13). It is insisted that the psalmist was praying for God to do something that was in harmony with God's nature to do. The total destruction of evil is God's prerogative. ". . . the wages of sin is death, . . ." (Rom. 6:23).

As there is a distinction between personal vindictiveness and administration of divine justice, the Psalms are an appeal to the justice of God to execute sentence upon the wicked. They are the backside of the coin: "Thy kingdom come, Thy will be done, on earth as it is in heaven" (Mt. 6:10). That state cannot come about without the destruction of evil. Paul ends the Corinthian letter: "If any one has no love for the Lord, let him be accursed. Our Lord, come!" (1 Cor. 16:22).

Even after considering these various ways of dealing with these Psalms, I would not find it right for a Christian to pray for the doom of any person. "Who are you to pass judgment on the servant of another? It is before his own master that he stands or falls . . ." (Rom. 14:4). One is not directed by the Spirit as the psalmists were. He has no infallibility in distinguishing the righteous from the wicked. The man he feels is the ultimate in wickedness may turn from his evil way; the chief of sinners may find mercy—Paul did. I find it more pleasant to follow Paul's admonition: ". . . I urge that supplications, prayers, . . . be made for all men" (1 Tim. 2:1).

PSALM 51:5(7): SHAPED IN INIQUITY, CONCEIVED IN SIN

> Behold, I was brought forth in iniquity;
> And in sin did my mother conceive me.

The heading of Psalm 51 assigns the psalm to the time of David's repentance after Nathan had confronted him with the knowledge of his great sin with Bathsheba. As a cry of confession of a tormented soul, fully conscious of his guilt and no place to go except to the Lord, it is unequaled in literature.

Verse 5, however, is one of the most perplexing verses

of the Bible.

Some interpreters have thought it expressed ideas of the sinfulness of sex relationships. But with the Lord providing for marriage at creation and giving the order to be fruitful and multiply (Gen. 1:28; 9:1; cf. 12:2), with children being a heritage from the Lord (Ps. 127:3), and with the forbidding of marriage being a sign of departure of the last times (1 Tim. 4:3), one cannot seriously argue that sex relations between a married couple are in any sense wrong. Sex relations and childbirth carried ritual uncleanness (Lev. 12:2, 5; 15:18), but ritual uncleanness is not to be identified with sin.

Another approach might argue that David is accusing his mother, saying that he is the result of a sinful act on her part. This view is unacceptable because there is not the slightest reason elsewhere to suppose that David was other than a legitimate son of Jesse and his lawful wife, duly married to each other.

The most widespread view of the verse is that it teaches the doctrine of original sin. This view was subscribed to by many church fathers after the time of Augustine,[3] by the Protestant reformers, and by all who accept that doctrine. It is used by them as a proof text of their position. Mitchell Dahood comments: "All men have a congenital tendency toward evil."[4] The objection to this widespread interpretation does not arise from the wording of the verse itself (the KJV and ASV renderings of the verse are literal) but arises from its clash with Scripture's teaching of individual responsibility such as

[3]References are given in James K. Zink, "Uncleanness and Sin: A Study of Job XIV 4 and Psalm LI 7," *Vetus Testamentum* 17 (July 1967):354-61.

[4]Mitchell Dahood, *Psalms II. 51-100*, The Anchor Bible (Garden City, N. Y.: Doubleday, 1968), p. 4.

was expounded in Ezekiel 18. It also clashes with Jesus' statement: "Let the children come to me . . . for to such belongs the kingdom of heaven" (Mt. 19:14).

Despite all the discussion that has gone on in the past, I would like to argue that the psalmist is using poetic hyperbole in his statement, comparable to that one uses when in agony over his sins. He says, "I have never been any good!" Ringgren calls the statement "a strong expression—perhaps poetically exaggerated—of the psalmist's feelings of being entirely and totally sinful."[5] His consciousness of the contrast between his condition and that which the Lord demands is made clear in verse 6: "Behold, thou desireth truth in the inward being; . . ." One finds comparable hyperbole to that used in the statement, "I am a worm, and no man; . . ." (Ps. 22:6). It is also used when one refers to trust in God: "From birth I have relied on you; . . ." (Ps. 71:6, NIV), or ". . . thou didst keep me safe upon my mother's breasts" (Ps. 22:9[10]). Paul uses comparable language to the Psalm when he says, "For I know that nothing good dwells within me, that is, in my flesh . . ." (Rom. 7:18).

PSALM 58:3(4): ESTRANGED FROM THE WOMB, ASTRAY FROM BIRTH

> The wicked are estranged from the womb:
> They go astray as soon as they are born, speaking lies.

Like Ps. 51:5(7), this statement is poetic hyperbole stressing the wickedness of the wicked, comparable to

[5]Helmer Ringgren, *The Faith of the Psalmists* (London: SCM Press, 1963), p. 69.

". . . the imagination of man's heart is evil from his youth; . . ." (Gen. 8:21). If the statement were taken in the most literal way, it would come close to being a statement of original sin; but the difficulties already stated with Ps. 51:5(7) here also deter one from taking the statement literally. Rather than taking the passage in isolation, it should be thought of as the converse of what the psalmist says of himself:

> Upon thee was I cast from my birth,
> And since my mother bore me thou
> Hast been my God (Ps. 22:10[11]).
>
> Upon thee I have leaned from my birth;
> Thou art he who took me from my mother's womb.
> My praise is continually of thee (Ps. 71:6).

That is to say, the psalmist's trust in God has been lifelong. The wicked man's revolt has also been lifelong; for him rebellion has become second nature. Of Israel it is said by the prophet: ". . . from birth you were called a rebel" (Is. 48:8).

PROVERBS 22:6: TRAINING CHILDREN AND THEIR GOING ASTRAY

> Train up a child in the way he should go,
> And when he is old he will not depart from it.

It is quite possible that this statement is a generalization whose truth is not tarnished by the occasional exception found in application. We have no easy answer to the problem of life where men like Eli, Samuel, and David produced wicked sons. Though most of us do the best we know how, we are all too familiar with the sad lament: "I trained him to do right, but he grew up and went the other way." Is it possible that the proverb is wrong—that one can train a child in the way he should go, and that still he will go wrong?

A person is a very complex creature made up of his genetic inheritance from his parents and of the influence of his environment. There are some factors that are unchangeable; but Ezekiel 18 denies that there is a genetic ethical inheritance that cannot be changed either for the better or for the worse. It is not that the fathers have eaten sour grapes and the children's teeth are set on edge, but the soul that sins is the one that shall die.

It is said that in modern society the average father spends less than ten minutes a day with his children. Meanwhile, the children have had six hours of school and a multitude of hours on the television. It is a pretty hard battle to mold the child very much with that sort of time handicap.

Some of the problems we have with our children are the inconsistencies in our own personalities. While we sing that "Jesus is all the world to me," our homes, our clothes, our cars, our recreation, and our bank accounts all show that we are really materialistic. Our children catch what we are and what we do more easily than they catch what we think we are trying to teach.

Another of our problems is our inconsistency in dealing with the child. The father and the mother do not present a unified front, but allow the child to play one against the other. Today he can get by with what we punished him for yesterday. Instead of well-mended fences understood by both parties, our actions depend on the mood we are in at the moment. If we are at our wits' end, he catches punishment from us; if we are in a good mood, he gets by with what he does.

Life brings a lot of influences into play that one does not have much control over. That child of yours is going to marry someone you had no part in training. Work is going to take him into an environment you cannot control. He will associate with people you can do nothing about. You have him for perhaps eighteen years out of the eighty that he may live. All of these factors merely underscore the complexities of the training process. We should ask whether the training we are giving is actually equipping the child for the way he should go. One cannot lay out a program that will guarantee success. We lament: "It worked with my first child but completely failed with the second!" That experience should remind us that we are dealing with individuals who have to be individually trained—not with automatons. Our own lack of adaptability to the changing problem may be a key to our failure.

Looking back over a failure, one may not be able to put his finger upon the exact point where he went wrong. If he had the opportunity to do it over, he may not know how he would do differently. But after all, is the test of the success of the shipbuilder to be found in the fact that his ship floats in the drydock; or is it to be found in whether or not the ship hangs together and successfully floats out the storm?

PROVERBS 31:6-7: DOES THIS SANCTION SOCIAL DRINKING?

Palestine is a vineyard region whose abundant vines are mentioned in the earliest geographical allusion to the country—that of the Egyptian Pepi in 2300 B.C. Palestine's wine was noticed in 1900 B.C. by Sinuhe who said: "It had more wine than water." The Israelite spies brought back grape clusters (Num. 13:23). Wine is regularly included in Old Testament lists of Palestinian agricultural products (Gen. 14:18; Josh. 9:4, 13; 1 Sam. 25:18; Hos. 2:8, 22). It is not surprising that both the Old Testament and the New Testament reckon with drinking it. The psalmist says that wine is a creation of God that gladdens the heart of man (Ps. 104:15) and a maker of parables say that it "cheereth God and man" (Judg. 9:13). Jesus turned water into the wine said by the guests to be the best at the wedding feast (Jn. 2:1ff.), and Paul recommended that Timothy be no longer a drinker of water only, but that he take a little wine for his stomach's sake (1 Tim. 5:33).

At the same time, the dangers of drunkenness are warned against in both Testaments. "Wine is a mocker, strong drink a brawler; and whoever is led astray by it is not wise" (Prov. 20:1).

> Who has woe? Who has sorrow? Who has strife? Who has complaining? Who has wounds without cause? Who has redness of eyes? Those who tarry long over wine, those who go to try mixed wine. Do not look at wine when it is red, when it sparkles in the cup and goes down smoothly. At the last it bites like a serpent, and stings like an adder. Your eyes will see strange things, and your mind utter perverse things. You will be like one who lies down in the midst of the sea, like one who lies on the top of a mast. "They struck me," you will say, "but I was not hurt; they beat me, but I did not feel it. When shall I awake? I will seek another drink" (Prov. 23:29-35).

Isaiah warns that the priest and prophet err through strong drink (Is. 28:7), and Paul urges the Christian, "...

do not get drunk with wine, . . ." (Eph. 5:18), and that aged women be not enslaved to much wine (Tit. 2:3). He states that the deacon is not to be given to much wine (1 Tim. 3:8).

Prov. 31:6-7, which we are now considering, is a part of a caution given King Lemuel by his mother. Having warned him in verse 3 not to chase women, she next points out that kings and princes should not indulge in drunkenness lest they forget the law and pervert the justice due to any that are afflicted. Her caution reminds one of Noah's drunkenness (Gen. 9:21), that King Elah was murdered while he was intoxicated (1 Kings 16:9), that Ben-hadad of Syria was defeated by Israel while he was on a drinking spree (1 Kings 20:16), that Belshazzar was giving a feast when the handwriting appeared on the wall (Dan. 5:1ff.), that Ahasuerus hosted a feast when he lost Vashti (Esther 1:10-11), and that King Herod while feasting murdered John the Baptist (Mk. 6:21-25).

In biblical exegesis when one asks a question that the writer of the passage was not answering, he regularly obtains the answer he has already unconsciously accepted on some other basis. The passage becomes merely a proof text for him. Prov. 31:6-7 is no exception to that statement. Lemuel's mother is not discussing whether social drinking is right or wrong. The purpose of her statement is to warn the ruler against engaging in self-indulgence instead of attending to his duties. The ruler has better things to do than to anesthetize himself. It is not for him to dull his mind, damaging its capability of rendering judgment. The mother is saying to her son, "Wine is not for you; let someone else drink who needs it because of his pain or misery."

Interpreters are divided over whether verse 7 is a sarcastic cut at the attitude that considers drunkenness the quickest way out of a difficult situation (when in reality it only deepens one's inability to solve his problem), or whether it is a serious comment suggesting occasions when the use of a stimulant is helpful. Either way, there is no encouragement for developing a drinking habit.

We all grant that the man in pain can be relieved with a shot of morphine. In preparation for an operation, a person is given what the nurses call "a happy shot." All operations are done under anesthesia. When calamity strikes, a person who has experienced an unbearable shock is given a sedative. In a world with less refined medicine than ours, a wound might be treated with oil and wine (Lk. 10:34). These above-mentioned conditions are the types of situations where Prov. 31:6-7 suggests that wine—a sedative of the ancient world—might be helpful:

> Give strong drink to him who is perishing,
> And wine to those in bitter distress;
> Let them drink and forget their poverty,
> And remember their misery no more.

It was not uncommon to offer a sedative to a condemned man. Such was offered to Jesus at his crucifixion, but he rejected it (Mt. 27:34; Mk. 15:23). Any thinking person would grant that there is a vast ethical difference between taking a sedative to relieve extreme distress and drowning one's cares in wine or other strong drink.

In our society, the effects of social drinking are all bad. One may say, "I can control my drinking," but the fact is that a large percentage of the alcoholics started on their path by social drinking. The social drinker ignores the effect his example may have on those about him and his responsibility for them. It is undeniable that automobile accidents, illicit sex, and crimes are made more frequent and serious by people who have relaxed their sensibilities by alcoholic drinks. The person who has put the kingdom of God first can find better ways to amuse himself and better ways to use his body.

6

Predicting the Virgin Birth

Isaiah 7:14

Every person who believes the New Testament believes that Is. 7:14 predicts the Virgin Birth. Every English translation on the market teaches that Is. 7:14 predicts the Virgin Birth, and any statement to the contrary is either a misunderstanding on the part of the one making it or is a prejudicial slander.

The question involved is not, Does Is. 7:14 predict the Virgin Birth? Mt. 1:23 plainly declares that it does. The question is, What does Matthew mean when he said, "All this took place to fulfill [*plērōthē*] what the Lord had spoken by the prophet"? One can attempt to impose a limiting definition on "fulfill" and can accuse all who differ with him of being unbelievers; but that does not establish the validity of his definition. Most of the discussion of the Virgin Birth question I have heard in our lectureships and which I have read in our journals ignores the problems of defining "fulfilled" and of establishing the validity of the definition being used.

Traditionally, beginning at least as early as the time of Tertullian (second to third century A.D.), it has been argued that "fulfilled" can be used in this verse of Matthew only to mean a literal fulfillment that had no predecessor in figure or any successor. However, Matthew, in 2:15, says that Jesus' coming out of Egypt fulfills a statement found in Hos. 11:1: ". . . out of Egypt I called my son." Matthew, here, uses the same Greek word that he uses in 1:23. In its setting in Hosea, the passage is talking about the Exodus under Moses. Matthew is telling us how that event prefigured the coming of Jesus out of Egypt. Later in 2:18, Matthew uses the same Greek word with "Rachael weeping for her children . . ." about a statement in Jer. 31:15 which, in its setting, plainly refers to the Babylonian exiles. That event prefigured the weeping of the people of Bethlehem over their children.

With two indisputable examples of how Matthew used "fulfilled" in the birth stories to mean a typical fulfillment, why has one denied the faith if he thinks Matthew uses a third (i.e., Is. 7:14) in exactly the same way? Why should one try to pour the Lord and Matthew into his mold of definition?

As Isaiah told Hezekiah that the sign (the same word used in Is. 7:14) that the Assyrian danger would pass was that in three seasons cultivation would be going on (Is. 37:30)—that is, the sign was a span of time measured by three seasons—so Isaiah told Ahaz that in the time it takes a woman to produce a child (nine months), plus the time required for a child to learn right and wrong, the danger Ahaz was afraid of would pass. The sign is the span of time involved. The name Immanuel is given the child to symbolize the help the Lord gave in giving the deliverance. This term is used (not as a name) in this way in Is. 8:10.

Matthew, then, tells us that the Lord was revealing more in that passage of Isaiah than one would see if he had heard the statement unaided (as Ahaz did) or if he read it unaided. The birth involved in that span of time prefigured the birth of Jesus. Jesus was virgin born and is the only person in history to be so born in the technical sense in which we understand "virgin"—that is, one born without a human father.

The strength of this approach to the question of the Virgin Birth is that it gives a logical solution to every problem of Is. 7:14. It interprets the passage in its context; it shows how the statement made could have had meaning to Ahaz in his problem; and it does not make Isaiah say to unbelieving Ahaz, "Seven hundred years from now the Lord will do something that will prove you wrong." The Greek, Latin, and English translators have never consistently rendered *'almah* by one term in all its occurrences (Gen. 24:43; Ex. 2:8; Ps. 68:26; Prov. 30:19; Song 1:3; 6:8; Is. 7:14). While there are no cases in the Bible where this term is used for a married woman, the discussion has now shifted out to its use in the cognate Semitic languages where there are alleged cases that it refers to women not technically virgins.

The explanation given above shows how *'almah* means "a young woman," the sex opposite of *'elem* which is rendered "stripling" or "youth" in its two occurrences (1 Sam. 17:56; 20:22). The masculine and feminine terms are like "lad" and "lass" in English. Finally, this approach lets Matthew define his own use of "fulfilled."

This explanation is not in any sense a rejection of the Virgin Birth prediction. It is only a rejection of some people's definition of the word "fulfilled."

7

"From the Beginning It Was Not So"

Matthew 19:8

When discussing the question of divorce, Jesus and his questioners used different verbs in their exchange to describe the provisions Moses had made. In the Gospel of Matthew the questioners, speaking of the certificate of divorce (the *get* of rabbinic discussion which read, "Lo, thou art free to marry any man . . ."), use the verb "command" (*entellesthai*): Moses commanded to give a bill of divorcement. But Jesus, without mentioning the certificate, replies about divorce with the verb "permit" (ASV: suffer; *epitrepein*). *Entellesthai* (command) is in the New Testament in fifteen cases (including parallels) where authoritative commands are spoken of.[1] *Epitrepein* (suffer, permit) is used in permissive contexts in sixteen cases (including parallels) in the New Testament.[2]

Because of the marked contrast in the import of the two verbs, one would be tempted to make a great deal of the shift in verbs were it not that in the Gospel of Mark the use of the verbs is reversed. There (Mk. 10:3b), in the account of the same discussion, Jesus speaks of Moses' "command" (*entellesthai*); the questioners return with "permit" (*epitrepein*); and Jesus then continues speaking of "this commandment" (*entolē*) which, in this case, should be understood as legislation relative to divorce.

Despite one's inability to build a special case on the different verbs used in the exchange, it is clear from the

[1]Angels receive charge (Mt. 4:6; Lk. 4:10); Moses commanded the adulteress to be stoned (Jn. 8:5); and the disciple is commanded to observe what Jesus taught (Mt. 28:20). In the parable, the master commands the porter to watch (Mk. 13:34); the Father gave Jesus commandment (Jn. 14:31); we are Jesus' friends if we do what he commands (Jn. 15:14); and he commands that we love one another (Jn. 15:17). Following the resurrection, Jesus commanded the apostles (Acts 1:2); God commanded the Gentile mission (Acts 13:47); God commanded the covenant at Sinai (Heb. 9:20); and Jacob gave commandment about his bones (Heb. 11:22).

[2]The young man asks permission to bury his father (Mt. 8:21; Lk. 9:59); another asks to bid farewell to his house (Lk. 9:60); the demons receive permission to enter the swine (Mk. 5:13; Lk. 8:32); Pilate permits the body of Jesus to be buried (Jn. 19:38); Paul asks the tribune permission to speak and is granted it (Acts 21:39-40); Agrippa grants Paul permission to speak (Acts 26:1); the Centurion permits him to visit his friends at Sidon (Acts 27:3); and Paul was challenged to stay by himself in Rome (Acts 28:16). Women are not permitted to speak (1 Cor. 14:34) or to teach or have dominion over a man (1 Tim. 2:12). Paul hopes the Lord will permit him to spend time in Corinth (1 Cor. 16:7); and the writer of the Epistle to the Hebrews promises progress from elementary doctrines if God permits (Heb. 6:3).

context that Jesus uses the creation narrative (Gen. 1:27; 2:24) to describe God's plan for marriage and suggests that the divorce arrangement is a deviation from that plan—a deviation made in concession to man's refusal to conform to God's plan where one man and one woman were created for each other to be united for life. They become one. The first polygamous union specifically mentioned in the Bible is that of Lamech (Gen. 4:19). The earliest patriarchs were monogamous; and the monogamous concept of marriage forms the basis for the comparison of Israel as the bride of God and the accusation that her traffic with other gods is adulterous.

YOUR HARDNESS OF HEART

"Hardness of heart" (*sklērokardia*), which is in the New Testament only three times (Mt. 19:8; Mk. 10:5; 16:14), is a term created in the Septuagint to render the phrase "uncircumcision of the heart" (*'arlath lebhabh*; Deut. 10:16; Jer. 4:4; Sir. 16:10; cf. Acts 7:51). It is related to the adjective "hard-hearted" (*sklērokardios*; Prov. 17:20; Ezek. 3:7) and also related to the concept expressed in the phrase "stony heart" (*kardia lithinē*; Ezek. 11:19f.; 36:26). There are, furthermore, the expressions *pōrōsei tēs kardias* (hardness of heart; Mk. 3:5) and "thy hardness [*sklērotēta*] and impenitent heart" (Rom. 2:5). *Sklērokardia* is analogous to *sklērotrachēlia* (stiffnecked; Ex. 33:3, 5; Deut. 9:6, 13; Prov. 29:1; Acts 7:5). Philo of Alexandria[3] made a homily on *sklērokardia*: " 'Circumcise the hardness of your hearts' . . . that is, prune away

[3]Philo *The Special Laws* 1.305.

from the ruling mind the superfluous overgrowth sown and raised by the immoderate appetites of the passions and planted by belly, the evil husbandman of the soul."

"Hardness of heart" (*sklērokardia*) occurs in Greek, in 1 En. 16:3, in the T. Sim. 6:2, and in early Christian writers. It is the trait which prohibits repentance;[4] it is included in Christian characterizations of the reason for Jewish disobedience;[5] and it is that which keeps man from obeying God.[6]

From these data, it can be seen that "hardness of heart" as used by Jesus describes man's unwillingness to conform to the plan God had for him. Despite God's plan for marriage in which one man and one woman lived in union for their lives, the unscrupulous husband might drive out the unwanted wife leaving her helpless, might starve her, or might dispose of her by murder. She might be denied her conjugal rights of clothing, food, and sexual intercourse (Ex. 21:10). The woman might be driven out by her husband and then charged with adultery if she married another. A man or woman might have a series of mates and then go back to the first. In the face of such possibilities, Moses provided for the bill of divorce (*sepher kerithuth*; LXX: *biblion apostasiou*; cf. Is. 50:1; Jer. 3:8). The provision was a restraint for ruthless husbands who might discard their estranged wives at will. They must give them a bill of divorce which protected them against a suit of adultery; but the whole was a concession to man's hardness of heart.

The contrast between Jesus' assertion about the basis for the Mosaic provision and the position occupied by some later Jews (third century A.D.) is striking. Though

[4]Hermas *Vision* 3.7.6.
[5]Justin *Dialogue* 16.2; 45.3; 46.7; 137.1.
[6]*Acts of Thomas* 166.

many rabbis sternly denounced the evils of divorce,[7] others argued that the right of divorce was a special privilege granted to Jews by the Lord because of his favor toward them, but which he had not extended to the Gentiles.[8]

That God has allowed men to do that which pleased themselves rather than doing that which conformed to his will is to be seen in a number of Old Testament cases.[9] When people craved meat in the wilderness, they were given quail but were also given "a wasting disease" (Ps. 106:15). Insistent Balaam was permitted to go with Balak's messengers but was charged only to bless Israel (Numbers 22-24). He was motivated by the love of "the gain from wrong-doing" (2 Pet. 2:15). Though the complete question of the attitude of the Old Testament toward the kingship is a very debated question among Old Testament scholars, at least the reason for wanting a king in the days of Samuel—the desire "to be like all the nations"—is condemned (1 Sam. 8:5ff.). They had rejected God from being king over them; nevertheless, Israel got a king. It was a detraction from God's rule; his special relationship with Israel was being violated. God told them he had given them "kings in my anger and I have taken them away in my wrath" (Hos. 13:11). God is said to deceive the false prophet (Ezek. 14:9). The whole problem of God's action seems analogous to the principle announced by Ezekiel:

[7]R. Eleazar (A.D. 270), "If a man divorces his first wife, even the very altar weeps" (*T.B. Gittin* 90b). See also Amram, *The Jewish Law of Divorce*, pp. 32ff.

[8]H. L. Strack and Paul Billerbeck, *Kommentar zum Neuen Testament aus Talmud und Midrasch* (Munchen: C. H. Beck'sche Verlagsbuchhandlung, 1926), 1:312, 805.

[9]David Daube, "Concessions to Sinfulness in Jewish Law," *Journal of Jewish Studies* 10 (1959):1-13.

> . . . Any man of the house of Israel who takes his idols into his heart and sets the stumbling block of his iniquity before his face, and yet comes to the prophet, I the Lord will answer him myself because of the multitude of his idols (Ezek. 14:4).

Or again, there is the working of error sent by the Lord to those "who did not believe the truth but had pleasure in unrighteousness" (2 Thess. 2:12).

DIVORCE IN THE MIDDLE EAST

Divorce was practiced by the Semites long before the time of Moses. Its origin is lost in antiquity. In ancient Sumer, the earliest known city civilization, a man could divorce his wife on relatively light grounds; and, if she had no children, he could marry another.[10] The code of Lipit-Ishtar from the second millennium B.C. has divorce provisions (law 30)[11] and the laws of Eshnunna (law 59) also do.[12] In Babylon, as attested by the Code of Hammurabi (law 137),[13] the divorced wife who has borne her husband children must be given her dowry plus field and garden to care for her children. Marriage with another man was permitted.[14] If the woman has not borne children, she receives the dowry she brought with

[10]Noel Kramer, *The Sumerians* (Chicago, Ill.: University of Chicago Press, 1963), p. 78.

[11]James B. Pritchard, ed., *Ancient Near Eastern Texts Relating to the Old Testament* (Princeton, N.J.: Princeton University Press, 1950), p. 160.

[12]Reuven Yaron, *The Laws of Eshnunna* (Jerusalem: Magnes Press, 1969), pp. 137ff.

[13]G. R. Driver and J. C. Miles, *The Babylonian Laws* (Oxford, England: Clarendon Press, 1956), 1:290ff.

[14]Stanley A. Cook, *The Laws of Moses and the Code of Hammurabi* (London: Adam & Charles Black, 1903), p. 123.

her at the time of her marriage (law 138). If there was no dowry, she receives a mina of silver; or if the husband is a poor man, she receives a third of a mina of silver (law 139). The woman could sue for a divorce if neglected by her husband (law 142); but, if her husband proved that she was a bad wife, she could be thrown into the river—likely an effective deterrent to hasty demand for divorce on her part.

Marriage contracts from Alalakh in northern Syria provided for the possibility of divorce with a reduced financial settlement if the wife initiated the divorce.[15] Hittite law (laws 31-33) allowed the couple to agree to separate from each other.[16] According to Assyrian law (law 37), it was the husband's choice whether he gave his wife anything or not when he divorced her. A marriage contract from the nineteenth century B.C. permits either husband or wife to divorce.[17] We do not have a Ugaritic law code which would enable us to know the details of divorce procedure there. The Ugaritic myths do not directly mention divorce,[18] but there are recorded cases of divorce between Ugaritic and Amorite royal figures.[19] All of these various cases show that divorce was widely practiced among Israel's neighbors before the time of Moses.

[15]I. Mendelsohn, "Marriage in Alalakh," in *Essays on Jewish Life and Thought Presented in Honor of S. W. Baron*, ed. Joseph L. Blau (New York: Columbia University Press, 1959), pp. 352f.

[16]E. Neufeld, *The Hittite Laws* (London: Luzac & Co., 1951), pp. 146-47.

[17]Pritchard, *Ancient Near Eastern Texts*, p. 107.

[18]Adriaan van Selms, *Marriage and Family Life in Ugaritic Literature* (London: Luzac & Co., 1954), pp. 49-50.

[19]See Margaret S. Drower, "Ugarit in the Fourteenth and Thirteenth Centuries," in *The Cambridge Ancient History*, ed. I. E. S. Edwards, 3d ed. (Cambridge: University Press, 1975), 2:2:142; Loren R. Fisher, ed., *Ras Shamra Parallels* (Rome: Pontifical Biblical Institute, 1975), 2:121.

There is no law in the Old Testament that institutes the practice of divorce; it was an age-old and accepted custom.[20] The law does not command it or establish it as right. Information on pre-Mosaic customs within Israel itself is wanting; but it must be assumed that divorce was practiced. Abraham's dismissing Hagar is the first record of divorcing a wife (even if a secondary wife; Gen. 21:10ff.; cf. Gal. 4:30f.). In Old Testament phraseology, the divorced woman (the *gerushah*—that is, the driven out one; Lev. 21:14; 22:13; Num. 30:9; Ezek. 44:22) has a lot that is not admirable (cf. Is. 54:6). In some cases she returned to her father's house (cf. Lev. 22:13). It may be assumed that some such formula as "she is not my wife and I am not her husband" (cf. Deut. 21:14; Hos. 2:2) was used. The law of Moses placed limitations on the existing practice. The privilege of obtaining a later divorce was forbidden the man who engaged in premarital intercourse with an unbetrothed woman whom he was then forced to marry (Deut. 22:28-29). Divorce was also forbidden the man who falsely accused his bride of premarital unchastity (Deut. 22:13ff.). The priest was forbidden to marry a divorced woman (Lev. 21:7, 14; Ezek. 44:22), but the priest's divorced daughter without children could be supported from her father's income which he derived from his holy occupation (Lev. 22:13). The divorced woman was considered legally responsible for her actions; her vow was considered binding on her (Num. 30:9). The matter of Deut. 24:1-4 will be considered later.

Other than the expelling of foreign wives at the period of the return from the Exile (Ezra 10; Neh. 13:23f.), the matter of divorce is largely left undiscussed in the Old

[20]Z. W. Falk, *Hebrew Law in Biblical Times* (Jerusalem: Wahrmann Books, 1964), pp. 154-57.

Testament. An exception is the bold declaration in Malachi,

> So take heed to yourselves, and let none be faithless to the wife of his youth. "For I hate divorce," says the Lord the God of Israel, . . . (Mal. 2:15b-16).

It is from this late passage that the true attitude of God toward divorce is to be found.

Continuation of the divorce problem within Judaism through the intertestamental years can be seen from the records of the Elephantine community in the fifth century B.C. which allowed either party of the marriage to dissolve the marriage without establishing any grounds in matrimonial offense. The husband had to return his wife's dowry and had to give her all her possessions.[21] Still later there is the "easy divorce" atmosphere of the first century where indeed divorce is "for every cause." Ecclesiasticus advised: "If she go not as thou wouldst have her, cut her off from thy flesh, and give her a bill of divorce, and let her go" (Sir. 25:26). Philo of Alexandria speaks of divorce "under any pretence whatever";[22] and Josephus, himself a divorced man,[23] said, "He who desires to be divorced from the wife who is living with him for whatsoever cause—and with mortals many such may arise. . . ." Finally, there is divorce evidence from the second century A.D. Murabba'at Papyrus.[24]

[21]Reuven Yaron, *The Law of the Aramaic Papyri* (Oxford, England: University Press, 1961), pp. 53ff.

[22]Philo *The Special Laws* 3.30-31.

[23]Josephus *Life* 75; *Antiquities* 4.253.

[24]J. T. Milik, "Contrat de Mariage, en Araméen (117 ap. J.-C.?)," in *Discoveries in the Judean Desert II, Les Grottes de Murabba'at,* ed. P. Benoit, J. T. Milik, and R. de Vaux (Oxford, England: Clarendon Press, 1961), pp. 110-13.

DEUTERONOMY 24:1-4

From this survey of the high points in divorce practices in the Middle East, it becomes clear that the providing for divorce cannot be the intention of the instruction in Deut. 24:1ff., which is the passage that Jesus' questioners brought up for discussion. Divorce was already being practiced in Israel long before the pronouncement of Deuteronomy was given. Moses merely set limitations, mentioning first the bill of divorce which protected the divorced wife from a later accusation of adultery. The bill terminated the marriage. Though we have no information on the origin of this practice, the giving of such bills is further alluded to in Is. 50:1 and Jer. 3:8.

The Deuteronomy passage is in the form of a casuistic law, many examples of which are in Ex. 21:1-6. The "If a man . . ." or "When a man . . ." law contains a protasis in which the hypothetical situation is described in a conditional construction. The protasis is then followed by an apodosis in which the applicable law is announced. In Deut. 24:1-4 the protasis ("When a man . . ."—*ki yiqqach* . . .) continues through the first three verses in a series of three hypothetical conditions; and the apodosis, introduced by "then" (RSV), is reached only in verse 4.[25] The RSV correctly reflects this structure. The KJV and ASV unfortunately give the first three verses a jussive force and, thereby, invite the reader to assume that they are commands. In the apodosis at verse 4, a grammatical form suitable to an absolute and permanent prohibition

[25]S. R. Driver, *A Critical and Exegetical Commentary on Deuteronomy*, International Critical Commentary, 3d ed. (Edinburgh, Scotland: T. & T. Clark, 1902), pp. 269-73; Martin, "The Forensic Background to Jeremiah III.1," pp. 82-92.

is given: "her former husband, who sent her away, may not take her again."

Two terms deserve special notice in the passage. The first, "to send away" (*shillech*), is the usual Hebrew word for "divorce" (v. 4; Deut. 22:19, 29; Is. 50:1; Mal. 2:16). The second term is "defile," which is the same term used elsewhere for the results of adultery (Lev. 18:20; Num. 5:13-14, 20); hence, the woman's relationships must be in some sense considered adulterous. Elsewhere, the land of Palestine is said to be defiled by the immoralities of its inhabitants (Lev. 18:25, 28; 19:29; Num. 5:3; Jer. 3:2, 9; Hos. 4:3).

The really crucial question in Moses' ordinance is that of the purpose of the ordinance. This question must be determined by the wording of the passage itself since the theme is not discussed elsewhere in the Old Testament. The intent of the passage does not seem to be to initiate or to prescribe the granting of divorce. The fact that divorce is practiced is assumed. The topic the passage discusses is whether or not the divorced woman can return to her first husband if her second husband dies or if he divorces her. Moses says that she cannot—a fact later recognized in the book of Jeremiah: "If a man divorces his wife and she goes from him and becomes another man's wife, will he return to her? Would not that land be greatly polluted?" (Jer. 3:1; cf. Is. 54:6f.).

In other words, the legislation of Moses is a limitation on divorce—not a provision for it. The purpose of the law was to prohibit the remarriage of a divorced woman to her first husband after she had been "defiled" by a second marriage, even though the second husband was dead. These are the only specifically regulative statements in the entire four verses. A Babylonian law also prohibited the husband to have intercourse with his divorced wife.[26] Rabbinic regulations later continued the prohibition for Jewish people.[27] The husband's giving the woman a bill of divorce (*sepher kerithuth*) is coincidental to the major theme of the passage. It is obvious that the giving of the bill was already a practice at the time, and it is taken for granted that it is handed to the wife. It enabled her to prove that she was divorced. It prevented the husband from later claiming rights over this ex-wife.

> When a man takes a wife and marries her, if then she finds no favor in his eyes because he has found some indecency in her, and he writes her a bill of divorce and puts it in her hand and sends her out of his house, and she departs out of his house, and if she goes and becomes another man's wife, and the latter husband dislikes her and writes her a bill of divorce and puts it in her hand and sends her out of his house, or if the latter husband dies, who took her to be his wife, then her former husband, who sent her away, may not take her again to be his wife, after she has been defiled; for that is an abomination before the Lord, and you shall not bring guilt upon the land which the Lord your God gives you for an inheritance (Deut. 24:1-4).

Despite what seems to be the rather clear intent of the law, by the first century the rabbis had come to consider that Moses in the law in regulating divorce was giving it recognition and was stating the basis on which a divorce could be given. They found the expression "some unseemly thing" (*'ervath dabhar*; LXX: *aschemon pragma*), which occurs only one other time in the Old Testament (Deut. 23:14[15]), to be the key phrase of the passage; but

[26]Cook, *Laws of Moses*, p. 124.

[27]Mishnah *Gittin* 4:7, 8; Philo *The Special Laws* 3.30-31; Josephus *Antiquities* 4.153.

here they parted ways. The school of Shammai put emphasis upon *'ervath* (uncleanness) which occurs in Old Testament settings dealing with lewdness, and they then concluded that lewd behavior (including sexual immorality) on the part of the wife was a basis for a divorce. They were engulfed in a problem of which they seemed unaware since the law actually said that the adulterous woman was to be stoned—not divorced (Deut. 22:22). However, though the case of the woman taken in adultery is reported in the Gospel of John (7:53ff.), there is reason to believe that the death penalty was not rigidly applied in the first century.

The school of Hillel, on the other hand, insisted that *dabhar* (thing) was the more crucial word in the Deuteronomy passage and from it concluded that if the wife was lacking in any way (for example, if she burned the bread), her husband could divorce her. Much later Rabbi Akiba entered the discussion and insisted that "if she finds no favor in his eyes" is the determinative phrase, and concluded that a divorce could be given if one found another woman more beautiful than she.[28]

Attention has been brought to a new factor in the divorce discussion of the first century with the publication of the Dead Sea Scrolls. It would appear that the Qumran community opposed divorce entirely. In the *Temple Scroll* it is said of the king:

> And he shall not take in addition to her another wife, for she alone shall be with him all the days of her life; and if she dies, he shall take for himself another [wife].[29]

Furthermore, the treatise called the *Cairo Damascus*

[28]Mishnah *Gittin* 9:10.
[29]11 *Q Temple* 57:17-19.

Document argues against polygamy by an appeal to Genesis:

> The builders of the wall . . . have been caught in unchastity in two ways: by taking two wives in their lifetime, whereas the principle of creation is "Male and Female he created them"; and those who entered the [Noah's] ark "two by two went into the ark." And concerning the prince it is written: "He shall not multiply wives for himself" (CD 7:1-3).[30]

"FROM THE BEGINNING"

With no interest in taking sides in rabbinic disputes, Jesus expounded to his questioners the will of God concerning marriage. Any deviation from the permanent type of union created at the beginning was a step downward. Man ought to follow the divine ideal, not a compromising concession made to sinfulness. By coincidence, of these cases of current discussion, it seems that Jesus was nearer the position of the school of Shammai than that of Hillel. He announced that there must be a valid reason for divorce if remarriage was to take place—there must be the cause of fornication (Mt. 5:32; 19:9). Divorce was not to be "for every cause" as the questioners suggested. Divorce was an evil custom arising from a degenerate people. God did not intend it that way. The statement of Deuteronomy was not to be discussed as a valid basis for divorce. The expression "from the beginning" (Mk. 10:6; cf. 13:19) should be understood in the sense of "from the beginning of creation" (cf. Rom. 1:20; 2 Pet. 3:4).

[30]R. H. Charles, *Apocrypha and Pseudepigrapha of the Old Testament* (Oxford, England: Clarendon Press, 1913), 2:810.

Though God had at the creation said that it was not good for man to be alone (Gen. 2:18), and though Paul later listed the demand of celibacy as a sign of departure from the faith (1 Tim. 4:3), the disciples' reaction to the rigidity in the marriage relation stated by Jesus was to raise the question if it would not be better to remain unmarried (Mt. 19:10); that is, to remain unmarried rather than to be bound until death to an unwanted though sexually faithful wife. Jesus' reply is that the teaching applies to those capable of marriage (Mt. 19:11-12). Though the rabbis taught that marriage was a duty,[31] Jesus noted that some might choose the single life "for the sake of the kingdom of heaven."

In the exchange over divorce wherein Jesus' opponents had attempted to play a later regulation against an earlier pronouncement—the statement of Deuteronomy as they interpreted it against the statement of Genesis—Jesus insisted that the reverse was the proper procedure. God's intent for marriage is to be found in Genesis where it is said that God made them male and female and said that a man should leave father and mother and cleave to his wife. The ideal is not found in the limitation placed on divorce in Deuteronomy. It is interesting to observe that these are the only two Old Testament passages considered in New Testament discussion of divorce. The passage from Deuteronomy is alluded to in Mt. 5:31; 19:6f.; and Mk. 10:4-5.

Jesus uses a type of argumentation also later used by Paul when Paul explained how the law fit into God's scheme. The law which came 430 years later could not negate God's promise to Abraham that in his seed all families of the earth would be blessed (Gal. 3:17; cf. Gen.

[31]Mishnah *Yebamoth* 6:6.

12:3; 17:8)—a promise that said nothing of the necessity of keeping the law. A new condition could not later be added to the promise. With Adam and Eve as the only pair at creation, divorce was out of the question. Their bond could not be dissolved. In Jesus' argument, the fact that Moses provided for a bill of divorce and limited remarriage could not change God's original plan for marriage in which a son left his father and mother and became one flesh with his wife. The original plan remained that situation which was pleasing to the Lord. By implication, each married couple should be as Adam and Eve—in their union they became one and what God has joined, man is not to put asunder. Only death itself should dissolve the bond:

> Thus a married woman is bound by law to her husband as long as he lives; but if her husband dies she is discharged from the law concerning the husband. Accordingly, she will be called an adulteress if she lives with another man while her husband is alive. But if her husband dies she is free from that law, and if she marries another man she is not an adulteress (Rom. 7:2-3; cf. 1 Cor. 7:39).

In a very similar teaching Paul elsewhere stated: ". . . that the wife not separate from her husband (but if she does, let her remain single or else be reconciled to her husband)—and that the husband should not divorce his wife" (1 Cor. 7:10-11). Paul demands that even if there is separation, the possibility for reconciliation must be kept open. Divorce is forbidden. Paul states his case as a word of the Lord.

CONCLUSION

From Jesus' words certain conclusions relevant to the current-day divorce problem must be drawn by all those who are concerned with the will of God for themselves. First, counselors should justify the demand they sometimes make that the divorced pair after leaving second or later marriages should go back to their first union—the very thing the regulation of Moses was designed to forbid (Deut. 24:1f.; Jer. 3:1f.). Mohammed[32] declared that which Moses had forbidden Jews to be proper for Muslims; but how does one know that Christian people today should do that which Moses said was an abomination to the Lord? Is there a biblical passage that reverses this demand?

Second, laws of states formed to conform to the majority will, whether they permit "no fault" divorce or divorce for any of the multiplicity of causes various states recognize, cannot be taken as expressions of the divine will. Regulations of churches representing compromises with man's sinful desires cannot be trusted for guidance in marital problems by members of the church the Lord established. They should attempt to conform to the divine purpose: "Thy will be done on earth as it is in heaven." It is clear that the marriage union in God's intention is permanent, indissoluble except by death. Those who divorce—sad as the case may be—have failed in the purpose God has in their union.

Third, the whole discussion should shift its focal point off hypothetical (or actual) questions of possible grounds for divorce and remarriage and focus it for each couple on the simple question, "How can we in our own bodies

[32]Qur'an *Sura* 2.

and in our own lives realize the purpose that God had for us in creating marriage?" The discussion should get us off the question, "How can we circumvent God's purposes?" In no other way can the divorce problem be effectively dealt with.

8

"This Commandment"
Mark 10:5

The hypothetical form of law does not authorize or approve the act that is described in the protasis of the law. For example, the law "If a man steals an ox or a sheep, and kills it or sells it, he shall pay five oxen for an ox, and four sheep for a sheep" (Ex. 22:1) does not authorize or permit either the theft of an ox or sheep or the sale of them. It recognizes that such acts happen and regulates them. The enactment of the law is, ". . . he shall pay five oxen for an ox and four sheep for a sheep." The law "If a man is found stealing one of his brethren, the people of Israel, and if he treats him as a slave or sells him, then that thief shall die; so you shall purge the evil from the midst of you" (Deut. 24:7) does not authorize or permit kidnaping or the sale of the one kidnaped. It recognizes that these acts happen; but the enactment of this law is, ". . . then that thief shall die; so you shall purge the evil from the midst of you."

The laws about rape (Deut. 22:23-29) lay out the conditions of the situation. One situation is:

> If there is a betrothed virgin and a man meets her in the city and lies with her, then you shall bring them both out to the gate of that city, and stone them to death with stones, the young woman because she did not cry out for help though she was in the city, and the man because he violated his neighbor's wife; so you shall purge the evil from the midst of you (vv. 23-24).

This law neither provides for nor approves of rape. It recognizes that rape happens and regulates it. God is responsible for these laws, and Moses wrote them; but God did not command, approve, or permit the acts being regulated.

These three laws (and many others in Exodus 22ff.) are exact parallels in form to that of Deut. 24:1-4. The enactment of Deut. 24:1-4 is so "her former husband, who sent her away, may not take her again to be his wife, after she has been defiled." Moses wrote the conditions, but in doing so only recognized what was likely to happen.

A real difficulty in the way of this interpretation for many people is the conversation between Jesus and the Pharisees reported in Mt. 19:7-8 and Mk. 10:2-5. In both passages, there is an alternation of verbs used by the questioner and the answerer. In Mt. 19:7-8, the people say, "Moses commanded" (*entellein*); and Jesus answered, "Moses permitted" (*epitrepein*). This answer gives no difficulty to the above stated interpretation of Deut. 24:1-4. The people express the attitude toward divorce otherwise known to have been held by Jews of this period; but, by his choice of verbs, Jesus could be correcting his questioners—God "permitted" rather than "commanded." Jesus also makes quite clear that, whatever Deut. 24:1-4 means, divorce was not God's plan: "From the beginning, it was not so."

In Mk. 10:2-5, the use of the verbs is the opposite to that in Matthew. Jesus asks what Moses "commanded"; they answer, "Moses permitted." Then Jesus comes back (v. 5) to say, "he wrote you this commandment" (*entolē*). For the person who follows only the English versions, there seems no escape from the conclusion that divorce and the bill of divorce are commands of Moses. He must conclude that the conditions listed in Deut. 24:1-4 have the force of a command. However, were he to study more diligently the implications of *entolē*, he might conclude otherwise.

In the seventy-one occurrences of the noun *entolē* (commandment) and the eleven occurrences of the verb *entellomai* (command), I have not found a single case where either word designates an optional privilege as it is commonly assumed that it does in Mk. 10:9. *Entolē* most often designates laws, orders, or instructions to be obeyed. The most frequent usage is in a phrase like "keep his commandment." The one who contends that Jesus is speaking of divorce as an optional privilege which has been granted has to argue for a special and unique meaning for *entolē* and *entellomai* in the divorce passages.

The understanding that divorce was instituted by Moses as a concession to human weakness—an interpretation taken over by the church from Judaism—was the basis for the Latin, the KJV, and the ASV renderings of

Deut. 24:1-4, causing the translators to give a jussive force: "that he shall write her a bill of divorcement, and give it in her hand, and send her out of his house." The phrase is likely not a jussive one in Hebrew or in Greek but is only one item in the series describing the situation which is to be regulated. Our dependence on these translations (KJV; ASV) makes it extremely difficult for our minds to function in any other pattern than that which they set. We can hardly ask whether the concession hypothesis is actually biblical, or whether it is an erroneous way, though long hallowed, of trying to understand what Jesus was saying about the hardness of heart.

There is no question that Moses wrote the conditions as well as the enactment. It is a gross misrepresentation to leave the impression that Mosaic authorship of the four verses of Deut. 24:1-4 is in any way under question. It is also a gross misrepresentation to leave the impression that there is any question of God's having stated the conditions there set forth. One is not questioning the Divine or Mosaic authorship of any of the hypothetical laws (the "If a man..." type) when he makes a distinction between the conditions and the enactments and asks what is being regulated. The only important question is whether or not the conditions have a jussive force, thereby being actions commanded, or whether they are indeed the conditions under which the law announced became applicable.

The argument, that had the divorce and the bill of divorce been wrong God (or Moses) would have said so, is what is known in logic as "begging the question" or "special pleading." The Old Testament does not explicitly state that plural marriage—which is subject to a law of the hypothetical type in Ex. 21:10—is wrong; yet such a marriage transgresses the marriage arrangement of Genesis 2. In the matter of divorce, how can God institute and approve that which he specifically says he hates (Mal. 2:16) and not be self-contradictory?

All people have already recognized that *entolē* as used by Jesus in Mk. 10:5 does not have the meaning we ordinarily attach to "commandment." Here, that which is "commandment" is only "permitted." One neither has to divorce nor give the bill of divorce. At the most, the man is permitted to divorce. By using *exestin* (lawful) and *epitrepein* (permitted), Jesus' questioners were claiming only that a privilege had been granted (Mk. 10:2, 4). If one would take only one more step and recognize that *entolē* can mean the whole "legislation," then I think the difficulty would disappear. The conditions specified in a piece of legislation are a part of the legislation. The writer states them, but he does not provide for their being done. He merely states that when these conditions exist, then his law is applicable.

This is the situation in Deut. 24:1-4. Moses is stating that when such conditions as those listed exist, a man cannot take the woman back. With this concept of the meaning of *entolē*, it is not necessary to assume as commentators, almost without exception, have that Jesus is saying that Moses made a concession to human weakness and provided divorce—an act which Mal. 2:16 proclaims that God hates. Jesus can be saying that Moses gave the legislation of Deut. 24:1-4 because of their hardness of heart. That hardness of heart had resulted in wife swapping, and Moses prohibited it (Deut. 24:1-4). It was a limitation on the freedom of divorce. But God's plan for marriage as a lasting union had not been changed.

In Mt. 19:8 and Mk. 9:5, Jesus used *pros tēn sklēro-*

kardian. Eduard Schweizer[1] argues that this phrase should be understood as "against your hardness of heart"; that is, that it is not a concession, but is a judgment on the people. That being true, Jesus is not saying that Moses weakened what had earlier been said about the permanence of marriage. Though this argument is counter to most of the commentaries I have seen on the Gospels, it fits the Hebrew structure of Deut. 24:1-4. In effect, Moses said, "You cannot take back the woman you divorced who has been married to another man."

[1]Eduard Schweizer, *The Good News According to Mark* (Richmond: John Knox Press, 1970), p. 203.

9

Baptizein and *Kōluein*
Mark 10:14

Since 1937, O. Cullmann has argued in three separate publications that the usage of *kōluein* in the New Testament in connection with Christian baptism reveals traces of an ancient baptismal formula.[1] The same type

[1]O. Cullmann, "Les traces d'une vieille formule baptismale dans le N.T.," *Revue d'Historie et de Philosophie religieuses* 17 (1937):424-34; *Urchristentum und Gottesdienst* (Zürich: Zwingli-Verlag, 1944), English trans. of 2d ed., 1950; *Early Christian Worship*, trans. A. Stewart Todd and James B. Torrance (Naperville, Ill.: n.p., 1953), p. 25; and O. Cullmann, *Baptism in the New Testament* (London: SCM Press, 1950), pp. 71ff.

of argument has also been advanced by J. Jeremias.[2]

This contention takes on particular importance in the exchange between Barth and Cullmann on infant baptism, where Cullmann argues that *kōluein* is a *terminus technicus*, forming a part of a baptismal liturgy of the early church. Before baptism was administered, one would ask: "What hinders 'so and so' from being baptized?" This question was answered, "There is no objection [*ouden exestin*]." Prior to heathen baptism, Cullmann asserts, "This is one of the essential and universal conditions demanded."[3] Cullmann next notices that *kōluein* also occurs in Mk. 10:13-16: "Let the little children come to me, do not hinder [*kōluete*] them." Upon this basis he offers this verse to help support the thesis which he thinks he has already established in his book, namely, that infant baptism is justifiable in the practice of the church.

The argument should be evaluated in two stages: First, does the evidence support the contention that *kōluein* formed a part of a baptismal formula? Second, does the occurrence of the word in Mk. 10:13-16 form a connection with the baptismal passages?

THE ARGUMENT FOR LITURGY CONSIDERED FROM STATISTICAL EVIDENCE

Baptizein

There are approximately twelve more or less detailed

[2]H. H. Rowley, review of *Die Kindertaufe in den ersten vier Jahrhunderten*, by J. Jeremias, in "Recent Foreign Theology," *Expository Times* 70 (July 1959):310.

[3]Cullmann, *Baptism*, p. 75.

reports of baptism in the New Testament:

1. Jesus (Mt. 3:13-17; Mk. 1:9, 10; Lk. 3:21-22; Jn. 1:33)
2. Pentecost (Acts 2:37-42)
3. The Samaritans (Acts 8:12)
4. Simon (Acts 8:13)
5. The Ethiopian (Acts 8:38)
6. Saul (Acts 9:18; 22:16)
7. Cornelius (Acts 10:48)
8. Lydia and her house (Acts 16:15)
9. The jailer (Acts 16:30ff.)
10. The Corinthians (Acts 18:8)
11. The twelve men in Ephesus (Acts 19:5)
12. The Corinthians (1 Cor. 1:14, 16)

There are numerous additional allusions to the act of baptism both as practiced by John, as commanded by Jesus, and as practiced by the early church. The root *baptizein* occurs some eighty times in the New Testament. Twenty-nine of these refer to John's baptism, six to Holy Spirit baptism, nine to the metaphor of suffering, four to the activity of Jesus' disciples during his personal ministry, two to the washing of pots and pans, one to the children of Israel under Moses, two to the baptism for the dead, and twenty-seven to the initiatory rite of the church.

Baptisma occurs in some twenty-two passages. Twelve refer to John's baptism. Five cases speak in the metaphor of suffering, and five cases refer to the rite of the gospel.

The noun *baptismos* is found in four passages, usually referring to washings. Only Heb. 6:2 could under any conceivable condition be connected with baptism.

Baptistēs as a name of John is found some fourteen times.

Out of all these baptismal passages, there are only four passages in which *kōluein* occurs. They concern the baptism of the Ethiopian, of Cornelius (two instances), and of Jesus. This leaves nine detailed narratives of New Testament baptism where there is no such connection. Put in another way, two-thirds of the narratives of baptism in the New Testament make no use of *kōluein*. All of the non-narrative allusions omit any reference to *kōluein*.

Kōluein

No less interesting are the statistics from *kōluein*. *Kōluein* occurs in the New Testament some twenty-three times in eighteen separate contexts, and *diakōluein* once, with an ordinary meaning of "hinder" or "prevent" such things as: preaching (Acts 16:6; 1 Thess. 2:16; 3 Jn. 10); paying tribute to Caesar (Lk. 23:2); entering the kingdom (Lk. 11:52); marriage (1 Tim. 4:3); speaking in tongues (1 Cor. 14:39); going on a journey (Rom. 1:13); casting out demons (Mk. 9:38); taking a coat (Lk. 6:29); and other varied activities. It occurs in the little children passage in the parallels: Mt. 19:14; Mk. 10:14; Lk. 18:16. Then there are the four passages in which baptism is under discussion which Cullmann notices: John would have hindered (Mt. 3:13f.); "What is to prevent my being baptized?" (Acts 8:36); "Can any one forbid water?" (Acts 10:47); and "Who was I that I could withstand God?" (Acts 11:17).

The Septuagint offers thirty-four occurrences of *kōluein* representing five Hebrew words: *kala'*, *mush*, *mana'*, *'asar*, and *shubh*. However, only once does it render *shubh* in the hiphil: "to cause to turn back" (Is. 28:6); once *mush* in the hiphil: "to remove" or "take away" (Mic. 2:4); and once *'asar*: "to restrain" or "to withhold" (Job 12:15). Of the passages where *kala'*—"restrain, shut up, withhold"—is translated, the thing withheld runs the entire gamut of possibilities: a sepulchre (Gen. 23:6); bringing gifts to the sanctuary (Ex. 36:6); prophesying (Num. 11:28); lips from praising God (Ps. 39; 40:9); feet from an evil way (Ps. 118; 119:101); and the departure of the spirit at death (Eccles. 8:8). In the two instances of *mana'*—"withhold" or "hold back"—a man is held back from bloodguiltiness (1 Samuel 25-26); and a woman is withheld from a man (2 Sam. 13:13).

Great variety is seen in the object hindered in the occurrences of *kōluein* in the Apocrypha: one hinders building the temple (1 Esd. 2:30; 6:6); the Lord hinders damage to his house (1 Esd. 6:33); Sarah is withheld from Tobit (Tob. 6:12); the demon is repelled (Tob. 8:3); appetites are restrained (Sir. 18:30); one is prevented from sinning (Sir. 19:28; 20:2); one forbids burnt offerings (1 Macc. 1:45); one is prevented from going to the country (1 Macc. 13:49); from entering a shrine (3 Macc. 1:13); one hinders the observance of the law (3 Macc. 3:2); one prevents taking a sum from the treasury[4]; God prevents eating food[5]; and one repels intruders.[6]

In classical and Hellenistic writers, *kōluein* stands to forbid persons to carry out an action and to forbid certain actions. The particular action forbidden varies widely. An example may be seen from Josephus: "What is there to prevent you from dispatching with your own hands your children and wives?" (*ti dē koluei tais heautōn chersin diachrēsasthai*).[7] This sentence is actually the

[4]4 Macc. 4:7.
[5]4 Macc. 5:26.
[6]4 Macc. 14:16-17.
[7]Josephus *War* 2.395; cf. *Antiquities* 16.51.

grammatical equivalent of Acts 8:36.[8]

There are ten occurrences of *kōluein* in second-century Christian literature: *Diog.* 4.3; 6.5; Ignatius, *Rom.* 4.1; Justin, *Apol.* 16.1; 30.1; *Dial.* 3.4; 17.4; Athenagoras 36.3; Tatian 29.2; and *Gospel of the Ebionites* (Epiph. 30.13). In each of these cases, the word has its ordinary meaning of "forbid," "hinder," or "prevent." Not in any of these, except in the *Gospel of the Ebionites* (which was mentioned by Cullmann), does it occur in a baptismal setting:

> And then it saith John fell down before him and said: I beseech thee, Lord, baptize me. But he prevented him saying: Suffer it: for thus it behoveth that all things should be fulfilled (Epiph. 30.13).

Putting the argument in the opposite way, no description of baptism around the second century uses *kōluein* except the *Gospel of the Ebionites*. Such descriptions are furnished us by the *Didache* 7 and by Justin Martyr (*Dial.* 61-65). Cullmann would have us to believe that a developing liturgical formula is to be seen in the New Testament which leaves absolutely no trace after the New Testament itself in the practice of the church.

In view of the wide variety of usages of *kōluein* in which no sign of a technical usage appears, both statistical evidence and the complete silence of second-century writers would make it seem quite speculative on Cullmann's part to argue that four occurrences in the New Testament are sufficient to support a case for a developing liturgical usage of the term.

[8]See Bauer, *Greek-English Lexicon*, p. 462; Henry George Liddell and Robert Scott, comps., *A Greek-English Lexicon*, rev. and aug. Henry Stuart Jones and Roderick McKenzie (Oxford, England: Clarendon Press, 1925-40), p. 1017.

DOES THE OCCURRENCE OF *KŌLUEIN* IN MARK 10:13 AND PARALLELS FORM A CONNECTION WITH THE BAPTISMAL PASSAGES?

The effort to connect Mk. 10:13ff. or its parallels with baptism can be traced all the way back to the time of Tertullian who opposes infant baptism, but at the same time alludes to the passage.

> The Lord does indeed say, "Forbid them not to come unto me." Let them "come," then, while they are growing up; let them "come" while they are learning, while they are learning whither to come; let them become Christians when they have become able to know Christ. Why does the innocent period of life hasten to the "remission of sins?"[9]

Calvin names the Mark episode "a defense against the Anabaptists."[10]

Cullmann readily admits that the passage does not originally speak of baptism:

> Though this account, which also contains the word *kōlüein* "hinder" does not speak of baptism but rather of the blessing of children by laying on of hands, yet we think it necessary to mention it here .... It is certain that originally it does not deal with baptism. . . . We will not indeed aver that the question of infant baptism was foreseen by Jesus; nor that the primitive church *invented* the occurrence of Mark 10:13-16 to justify infant baptism.[11]

[9]Tertullian *De baptismo* 18 (ANF 3:678).

[10]Cullmann, *Baptism*, p. 77, citing John Calvin, *A Harmony of the Gospels Matthew, Mark and Luke*, trans. T. H. L. Parker (Edinburgh, Scotland: Saint Andrew Press, 1972), 2:252.

[11]Cullmann, *Baptism*, pp. 76-78.

Nevertheless, Cullmann proceeds to argue that those who transmitted the story wished to call to the remembrance of Christians an occurrence by which they might be led to a solution of the question of infant baptism.

When analyzed, Cullmann's argument is equal to what in rabbinic thought would be called a *Gezera Shava* of the constructional type. A *Gezera Shava*, the second of the thirteen exegetical principles of R. Ishmael, is an argument construing laws with reference to each other so that certain provisions connected with one of them may be shown to be applicable also to the other. The form ordinarily is:

> Here it is said .... There it is said .... As here ... so there.[12]

By using this device, Hillel can argue from the fact that the daily offering was to be brought "in its due season" (Num. 28:2), which includes the Sabbath (Num. 28:10), that the Passover was to be kept "in its due season" (Num. 9:2), and that the Passover was to be offered even on the Sabbath.[13]

It is easy to see that the method can readily lapse into fallacy. In the Talmud this led to such restrictions as specifying that one of the terms must be seen superfluous if an analogy is permitted and that one must receive the analogy from the tradition rather than manufacturing it on his own in order to deduce new laws from Scripture.[14]

At its foundation, Cullmann's case does contain a *Gezera Shava: Kōluein* is in the baptism passages, and *kōluein* is in the child-blessing passage; hence, the child-

[12]M. Mielziner, *Introduction to the Talmud* (Cincinnati, Ohio: Block Printing Co., 1894), p. 143.

[13]Ibid., pp. 145-46.

[14]Ibid., pp. 150-52.

blessing passage can be connected with baptism. Cullmann, however, has not regarded either of the rabbinic restrictions. First, *kōluein* is not a superfluous word in either passage. Second, Cullmann has deduced from the analogy a new teaching which, by his own admission, was not originally in the passage.

The fallacy of the argument is all too obvious when one applies the same argument, which one has a perfect right to do, to the other passages where *kōluein* occurs. By this means, there is a connection between baptism and paying tribute to Caesar (Lk. 23:2); marriage (1 Tim. 4:3); taking a coat (Lk. 6:29); casting out demons (Mk. 9:38); and many other items. Shall we conclude that the church preserved the account of Paul's friends not being hindered (*kōluein*) to come to him (Acts 24:23) because the episode had in their mind some connection with baptism? Did the disciples baptize the man casting out demons in the Lord's name who would not follow them when they forbade (*kōluein*) him (Lk. 9:49)?

In modern logic, Cullmann's fallacy would be known as the fallacy of the undistributed middle. An example is: "All clowns are men, the class president is a man; therefore, he is a clown."[15] Putting Cullmann's assumption into this form it appears thusly: *Kōluein* is preserved by the church in connection with baptism. Blessing children is preserved in connection with *kōluein*; therefore, blessing children has to do with baptism.

One can only conclude that Cullmann has not given us a secure connection between child blessing and infant baptism.

[15]D. S. Robinson, *The Principles of Reasoning* (New York: D. Appleton-Century Co., 1947), p. 124.

10

The Christian and The Government

Romans 13:1-7

Rom. 13:1-7 is one of the few direct references in the Pauline corpus of letters to the Christian's duty to society outside the church.[1] Here only general principles are stated relevant to the problems that press upon the modern man most heavily. The duty of the Christian in an evil totalitarian state such as that under Hitler, the duty in the presence of tyranny and oppression, the right of voting in a democracy, the right and the duty of the Christian to be a magistrate, and the duty to bear arms

[1]When C. A. Scott, *Christianity According to Paul* (Cambridge: University Press, 1927), p. 232, states that it is the only reference, he is excluding the pastorals.

are not taken up. For this reason, these matters through the history of the church have been and continue to be debated.[2]

The sustained theological argument of the Epistle to the Romans—expounding the doctrine of salvation by faith and its unfolding in God's actions in history—fills chapters 1 through 11. The second part of the letter—chapters 12ff.—deals with practical problems confronting the Christian in his "spiritual worship" (*logikē latreia*).[3] These problems are a consequence of the actions of God discussed in the first part: the presenting of one's body as a living sacrifice, his relations with his brother, his attitude to the state, the *parousia* as a motive for moral conduct, and the need to exercise forbearance in matters where one is "weak" and another is "strong."

Why Paul dealt with the state at this particular spot is not clear.[4] Whether, as Calvin and others have supposed, the question arose out of a specific problem in Rome or not must remain conjectural. Certainly, at this period Palestine was seething with unrest that would burst into flame in a few short years in the tragic revolt of A.D. 66 resulting in the destruction of the Jewish state. Suetonius tells us that a few years earlier Claudius had expelled

[2]See J. Kosnetter, "Rom. 13:1-7: Zeitbedingte Vorsichtsmassregel oder Grundsätzliche Einstellung?" *Studiorum Paulinorum Congressus Internationalis Catholicus, 1961*, Analecta Biblica 17-18 (Rome: Pontifical Biblical Institute, 1963), 1:348-55, for a survey of some issues raised by the favorable view of the government taken by Paul in this passage.

[3]C. E. B. Cranfield, "Some Observations on Romans XIII: 1-7," *NTS* 6 (April 1960):241ff.

[4]The effort of James Kallas ("Romans XIII:1-7: An Interpolation," *NTS* 11 [July 1965]:356-74) to establish that this section is an interpolation is unconvincing because his basic assumptions are erroneous.

Jews from Rome for making disturbances with *Chrestus* as an instigator.[5] *Chrestus* is most likely to be understood as "Christ" and is a reflection of Jewish-Christian relations. In a few years, in A.D. 64, the persecutions of Nero would break over the church. What part, if any, these had to play in the writing of this letter we do not know. The section we are examining is a section bracketed on its two sides by an exhortation to love (Rom. 12:9-10; 13:8ff.).

CIVIL AUTHORITIES ARE FROM GOD

Just as Jesus reminded Pilate that he had no power except that given him from above (Jn. 19:11), so also for Paul, God is the ultimate source of all authority. Authorities are not an independent force of any sort. They are from God and are constituted by him.

The liveliest issue today on this matter is that raised by O. Cullmann when he argues that the plural phrase *exousiai huperechousai* should be translated "supreme powers" and be understood as angelic powers.[6] Cullmann admits that the context speaks of the state, but insists that this implies that the actual state authority is thought of as the executive agent of angelic powers and that this concept is the normal one for late Judaism and for the New Testament. Cullmann argues that Paul elsewhere always uses *exousiai* in this meaning; hence, for Paul the word in this passage must have a double

[5]Suetonius *Life of Claudius* 25.

[6]O. Cullmann, *Christ and Time* (Philadelphia, Pa.: Westminster Press, 1950), pp. 194ff.; *The State of the New Testament* (New York: Scribner, 1956), pp. 93ff. This case is further expounded with some modifications by C. Morrison, *The Powers That Be* (Naperville, Ill.: Allenson, 1960).

meaning: angels and state authorities as their representatives. He also argues that the same double meaning is to be found in 1 Cor. 2:8 where *archontes tou aiōnos toutou* occurs. These powers in the period between the resurrection and *parousia* of Christ are ministering spirits (Heb. 1:14),[7] subjected to the lordship of Christ and are in the service of Christ. At times, however, within this bond they express their former evil demonic nature. Cullmann feels that this view explains why the state may be praised in Romans, but condemned in 1 Corinthians 6 and in Revelation 13. Cullmann calls this total concept the "Christological foundation" of the state: both church and state are in the kingdom of Christ. The church knows it, but the state need not, insofar as it is a pagan state.

As early as the second century, Irenaeus denied the validity of a similar view and insisted that the theme at hand is civil authority.[8] Cullmann attempts to rebut on the basis that Irenaeus is objecting primarily to a dualism to which he is not subscribing. Cullmann's case has also drawn heavy fire from Brunner,[9] Leenhardt,[10] and others.[11] It is admitted to begin with that *archontes* may be both spiritual powers (Eph. 2:2) and earthly rulers (Acts 3:17),[12] and that *exousiai* likewise may be

[7]Notice that *leitourgos* and *diakonia* enter into this description (cf. Rom. 13:4, 6).

[8]Irenaeus *Adv. Haer.* 5.24.1.

[9]H. E. Brunner, *Justice and the Social Order*, trans. Mary Hottinger (London and Redhill: Lutterworth Press, 1945), p. 272.

[10]F. J. Leenhardt, *The Epistle to the Romans*, trans. Harold Knight (London: Lutterworth Press, 1961), pp. 328-29.

[11]See the bibliography in G. Stählen, "*Orgē*," in *Theological Dictionary of the New Testament*, ed. Gerhard Kittel, trans. and ed. G. W. Bromiley (Grand Rapids, Mich.: Wm. B. Eerdmans Publishing Co., 1971), 5:441, n. 401. Hereafter cited as *TDNT*.

[12]G. Delling, "*Archōn*," *TDNT*, 1:486f.

used each way.[13] But it seems unlikely in view of Col. 2:15 that Paul would be urging Christians to be in subjection to angelic powers.

Leaving the current controversy and returning to the major theme of the passage, we notice that Paul's declaration that *exousiai huperechousai* are from God has as its background similar declarations in the Old Testament. The prophets speak of the Assyrians as the "rod of God's anger" (Is. 10:5), of the Lord's raising up the Chaldeans (Hab. 1:6), of Nebuchadnezzar as God's servant to whom God has given the land and to whom people must submit (Jer. 25:9; 27:6-11; 43:10), and of Cyrus as the Lord's anointed (Is. 45:1; cf. 44:28). Ezra admonishes Israel to pray for the life of Darius and his sons (Ezra 6:10). God removes kings and sets up kings (Dan. 2:21; cf. 27, 38; 4:26, 28), and he rules in the kingdoms of men (Dan. 4:32).

Nor would these thoughts be unorthodox in Judaism. "The government of the earth is in the hands of the Lord, and over it he will raise up the right man for the time" (Sir. 10.4). "Your dominion was given you from the Lord" (Wisd. 6:3; cf. 1 En. 46:5; 2 Bar. 82:9). "No ruler attains his office save by the will of God."[14] Jeremiah had urged the exiles to seek the peace of Babylon and to pray to the Lord in its behalf (Jer. 29:7). Offerings were made in the temple for Antiochus IV Epiphanes (1 Macc. 7:33).

The rabbis—though our examples are later than Paul—would not have differed. R. Hanina (ca. A.D. 70) said: "Pray for the prosperity of the government since but for the fear of it one man would swallow the other

[13]W. Förester, "*Exousia,*" *TDNT,* 2:559ff. *Exousiai* for civil authorities is to be seen in Josephus *War* 2.350; Lk. 12:11; and Tit. 3:1.

[14]Josephus *War* 2.140.

alive."[15] Upon seeing a non-Jewish king, one should say: "Blessed be He that hath imparted of His glory to His creatures."[16] About A.D. 110, R. Jose b. Kisma said: "Knowest thou not that it is heaven that has ordained this [Roman] nation to reign? For though she laid waste His House, burnt His Temple, slew His pious ones and caused His best ones to perish, still is she firmly established!"[17] About A.D. 220, R. Shila in Babylon said: "Blessed is the All-Merciful who has made the earthly royalty on the model of the heavenly, and has invested you with dominion."[18] R. Judan (ca. A.D. 350) said: "He who is insolent toward a king is as though he were insolent toward the *Shechinah*."[19]

As unwelcome as these sentiments when applied to Rome were to the Zealots, and ineffective as they were in preventing the tragic revolt of A.D. 66-70 and in preventing many rabbis like Akiba from giving their blessing to the Bar Cochba revolt in A.D. 135, they nevertheless furnish an excellent background against which to consider Paul's assertion. The "Powers that be" (*hai de ousai*; v. 1) contains an evaluation of Rome.

Neither Jesus nor Paul could have been oblivious to wrongs done by the magistrate. It is inconceivable that the apostle is affirming the infallibility of the magistrate (Mk. 10:42; Lk. 22:25-26). The disciple was to expect to be brought before rulers and authorities (Lk. 12:11). In ignorance, authorities had crucified Jesus (Acts 3:17;

[15]Mishnah *Aboth* 3:2.

[16]*T.B. Berakoth* 58a.

[17]*T.B. 'Abodah Zarah* 18a.

[18]*T.B. Berakoth* 58a.

[19]*Gen. R.* 84:9; other examples are in Strack and Billerbeck, *Kommentar*, 3:303-4. Early Christian writers also reflect these views; cf. *1 Clement* 60; *The Martyrdom of Polycarp* 10:2.

4:27-28). Had the rulers of this age recognized God's wisdom they would not have crucified the Lord of Glory (1 Cor. 2:8). Paul had known imprisonment and had felt the lash of the magistrate—Jew and pagan—wielded unjustly (Acts 16:20ff.; 2 Cor. 11:24-25). But despite it all, the authorities are from God and are ordained of God. Any form of government is preferable to anarchy.

It has long been recognized that the major problem of this passage is faced when we ask if this teaching also applies to the diabolical state and when we ask what is the Christian's responsibility to such a state. Whether it be the Zealots or the most modern revolutionaries, men have always been able to convince themselves that it is God's will for them to change an unbearable situation. But is this self-delusion?

A second question is that of whether there is an essential difference reflected here from Paul's reluctance for Christians to go before a heathen court—"those least esteemed by the church" (1 Cor. 6:4)—and from his recognition that it was the authorities who crucified Jesus (1 Cor. 2:8). Is there a difference from the attitude reflected in the picture of Rome as the beast rising up out of the sea who receives *exousia* from the dragon (Rev. 13:1; cf. Lk. 4:6)?[20]

Paul, though he does not cite the passages, could not have been oblivious to Isaiah's concept that Assyria can exhaust its commission (Is. 10:12), that "The kings of the earth set themselves . . . against the Lord and his anointed, saying, 'Let us burst their bonds asunder, and cast their cords from us' " (Ps. 2:2-3), and that the nations may exceed their commission (Zech. 1:15). Yet the details of "what if" do not find exposition.

[20]Notice that even the beast is not an independent authority. His *exousia* over tribes and nations is given him (Rev. 13:7).

THE FUNCTION OF RULING AUTHORITIES

Paul sees the function of ruling authorities as threefold. First, there is the punishment of the evildoer. The ruler (*archōn*) is the "servant" (*diakonos*)[21] of God to execute wrath (*ekdikos eis orgēn*)[22] upon the evildoer and does not bear the sword in vain (v. 4). Though the sword was a symbol of authority, along with it went the *ius gladii*—the power to enforce the death penalty. The function of vengeance (*ekdikēsis*) and wrath (*orgē*) is forbidden the Christian in the preceding chapter (Rom. 12:17a, 19), but is here specified for the *archōn*. Dodd has pointed out that Paul does not consider the case of a successful rebel; a Roman citizen knew no successful rebels.[23] Paul's statement is clearly to say that the punishment meted out by the ruler is an example of God's wrath.[24]

Second, the ruler is a servant (*diakonos*) of God for your good.[25] It is striking to notice the repetition of *diakonos* in these two sections: *diakonos, ekdikos eis orgēn—diakonos eis to agathon*. Paul, though he suffered at the hands of some magistrates (Acts 16:20-24; 2 Cor. 11:25ff.), found the magistrates a protection against ill treatment and caprice at the hands of the Jews and pagans (Acts 18:12ff.; 19:38ff.; 22:25). Magistrates are on the side of righteousness. If you do good, you have praise from them (cf. 1 Pet. 3:13).

Third, the ruler is a minister (*leitourgos*) of God to

[21]H. W. Beyer, "*Diakonos*," *TDNT*, 2:88ff.

[22]*Ekdikos* occurs in the New Testament here and in 1 Thess. 4:6, but the root *ekdikei* is not rare. See G. Schrenk, "*Ekdikos*," *TDNT*, 2:442f.

[23]C. H. Dodd, *Epistle of Paul to the Romans* (New York and London: Harper, 1932), p. 204.

[24]Cf. Is. 10:5-16 for a similar concept of Assyria as the rod of God's anger.

[25]Paul assumes the reader to be in the class who submit.

collect tax and to receive reverence and fear. "For this very thing" (*eis auto touto*) may refer to tax gathering; that is, God has ordained the means by which rulers operate.[26] *Leitourgia* is a word of diverse uses. Beginning as a service voluntarily undertaken by a citizen, it became a service laid upon a citizen who possessed more than three talents. It may be a service rendered man to man, as the collection for the saints (Rom. 15:27; 2 Cor. 9:12) or the service of Epaphroditus to Paul (Phil. 2:17, 30). It may be a religious service as that of Zechariah (Lk. 1:23; Acts 13:2) or such as the high priestly work of Jesus (Heb. 8:2, 6). Paul is *leitourgos* to the Gentiles (Rom. 15:16)—that is, as Athens sent out its *leitourgoi* to represent the state, Paul is sent by God to the Gentiles.[27] Some have seen the phrase in Romans as implying a priestly function for the magistrate,[28] but it would seem more likely that the last example cited furnishes the better parallel.[29]

THE DUTY OF THE CHRISTIAN

By heaping up words from the root *tassein*, the apostle creates an impact that emphasizes submission: "be

[26]Charles Hodge, *Commentary on the Epistle to the Romans* (1886; reprint ed., Grand Rapids, Mich.: Wm. B. Eerdmans Publishing Co., 1955), p. 409. An equally possible meaning is that the magistrate is a minister for the total services here described; see H. W. A. Meyer, *Critical and Exegetical Handbook to the Epistle to the Romans*, trans. John C. Moore et al. (Edinburgh, Scotland: T. & T. Clark, 1879), p. 283.

[27]W. Barclay, *A New Testament Wordbook* (New York: Harper, 1955), pp. 74-76.

[28]A. Richardson, *An Introduction to the Theology of the New Testament* (New York: Harper, 1958), p. 297; Meyer, *Commentary*, p. 283.

[29]See W. Grundmann, "*Leitourgia*," *TDNT*, 3:620f.

subject" (*hupotassesthai*), "ordained" (*tetagmenos*), "resist" (*antitassomai*), and "ordinance" (*diatagē*). "Be subject" (*hupotassesthai*) is a general word found in the passive thirty times in the New Testament: the church is subject to Christ (Eph. 5:24); the spirits of the prophets are subject to the prophets (1 Cor. 14:32); Christians are to be subject to each other (1 Cor. 16:16; Eph. 5:21). Three occurrences of this word deal with responsibility to rulers (Rom. 13:1; Tit. 3:1; 1 Pet. 2:13). Of these, Tit. 3:1 differs from our passage in also adding a more specific Greek word for obedience—*peitharchein*.[30] Paul's statement offers an interesting parallel to the later dictum of R. Samuel (ca. A.D. 254): "The law of the government is law."[31]

This duty of subjection falls upon all (*pasa psuchē*)[32] without exception. Paul attempts no complete bill of particulars of what is involved in *hupotassesthai*, but some items follow:

1. Doing good (*to agathon poiei*; Rom. 13:3). In verse 2, Paul with *hōste* deduces a consequence from his previous major assertion. Resistance to authorities is not only resistance to that which God has appointed (*diatagē Theou*), but will bring wrath (*orgē*) upon one. Right doing brings approval of the ruler (cf. 1 Pet. 2:14).

2. Payment of tax (*telos*) and tribute (*phoros*).[33] The verb construction *teleite* may grammatically be either a

[30]See Cranfield, "Observations," pp. 242-45.

[31]*T.B. Baba Bathra* 54b; *Baba Kamma* 113a.

[32]*Pasa psuchē* is here used for "person," a sense attached in the Old Testament to *nephesh* (cf. Gen. 14:21; 46:27), and means "everyone": Lev. 7:27; Acts 2:43; 3:23; Rom. 2:9; Rev. 16:3. See Walter Bauer, *A Greek-English Lexicon of the New Testament and Other Early Christian Literature*, rev. William F. Arndt, F. Wilbur Gingrich, and Frederick W. Danker, 2d ed. (Chicago, Ill.: University of Chicago Press, 1959), p. 902.

[33]Cf. Irenaeus *Adv. Haer.* 5.24.1.

statement or a command. This duty Paul introduces with *dia touto* "for this reason" to draw a deduction from his threefold basis for submission which he has just mentioned and which will be considered shortly.

Telos is ordinarily an indirect tax, custom, or duty (1 Macc. 10:31; 11:35)[34] which, other than in this pericope, is found once in the New Testament. Jesus instructed Peter to pay *telos* (Mt. 17:25).[35]

Phoros (RSV: revenue; NEB: toll), in contrast, is thought to be a direct tax[36] and occurs five times in the New Testament (Lk. 20:22; 23:2; Rom. 13:6-7).[37]

Unlike Judas, the Galilean who insisted that paying tax to Rome was treason to God,[38] Paul and Jesus (Mt. 22:21; Mk. 12:17; Lk. 20:25), using the same word for paying (*apodidonai*), granted Caesar what is Caesar's. Conforming became a point of honor with the early church.[39] Tertullian could boast that the empire gained more from Christian taxes than it lost from their refusal to support the temples.[40]

3. Rendering reverence. *Phobos* (fear or reverence) occurs forty-seven times in the New Testament and may convey either a sense of terror or reverence. It can be the bad man's emotion (Rom. 13:3) or the feeling of a slave (Rom. 8:15; Eph. 6:5). It made Joseph of Arimathea a secret disciple (Jn. 19:38); it caused the disciples to keep doors locked (Jn. 20:19); it keeps a man from showing whom he serves (1 Pet. 3:14); and it is forbidden the

[34]Josephus *Antiquities* 12.41.

[35]See Bauer, *Greek-English Lexicon*, pp. 819-20.

[36]1 Macc. 8:4, 7; Josephus *War* 2.403; *Antiquities* 14.203; *Apion* 1.119.

[37]See Bauer, *Greek-English Lexicon*, p. 872.

[38]Josephus *War* 2.108; *Antiquities* 18.1f.

[39]Irenaeus *Adv. Haer.* 5.24.1.

[40]Tertullian *Apol.* 42 (ANF 3:49).

Christian (1 Pet. 3:6, 14). It has torment and is cast out by love (1 Jn. 4:16, 18).

On the other hand, "fear of God" (*yirath 'elohim*) is one of the most frequent terms in the Old Testament to describe religion (cf. Is. 8:13; Acts 9:31; Rom. 3:18). This is the reverence of man in the presence of God. The term lays a basis for the contention that God is the object to whom *phobos* is due (Rom. 13:7). God is to be feared—one is to fear him who can destroy both soul and body (Mt. 10:28)—but is *phobos* exclusively his? Peter ascribes "fear" (*phobos*) to God and "reverence" (*timē*) to the king (1 Pet. 2:17), but that he intended to make a real distinction between *phobos* and *timē* cannot be established since the next verse ascribes *phobos* to the ruler. Human beings are proper recipients of *phobos*: the wife fears her husband (Eph. 5:33); the church receives Timothy with fear (2 Cor. 7:17). Though used in the sense of dread in verse 3, in verse 7 *phobos*, as in the examples just mentioned, should be understood in the sense of "reverence." The Christian should not withhold reverence from the one to whom it is due.[41]

4. Giving honor. *Timē*—"honor"—is found forty-three times in the New Testament for the honor shown masters (1 Tim. 6:1); rulers (1 Pet. 2:17); one another (Rom. 12:10); Christ (2 Pet. 1:17); or to God (Rev. 3:4; 1 Tim. 1:17; 6:16).[42] Hodge states that *phobos* and *timē* differ only in degree: The former expresses reverence to superiors, the latter respect to equals.[43] Paul would urge Christians to give the magistrate the honor his office

[41] A. Strobel, "Furcht, wem Furcht Gebührt: Zum profangriesschen Hintergrund zum Rm. 13:7," *ZNTW* 55 (1964):58-62, finds a Greek parallel demanding "fear" for the magistrate.

[42] See Bauer, *Greek-English Lexicon*, p. 825.

[43] Hodge, *Romans*, p. 409.

carries and in this would not differ from the teaching of the later rabbis.[44]

These last four duties are set forth in a summary verse which declares that every man (*pas*, i.e., all in authority) is to be given his due (*opheilē*) which is the term the Lord used in prescribing that Caesar is to have what is Caesar's. It is a debated question whether verse 8 continues the theme of verse 7 or whether it begins a new theme. But it is striking that it repeats that the Christian is to owe (*opheilein*) no man anything, which word seems to tie in with the preceding verse. The Christian is not to evade his obligation to authorities.

Earlier the point was made that this pericope does not pretend to be a *summa* of one's obligation to the authorities. For example, the duty of prayer does not come into view here but is expounded elsewhere (2 Tim. 2:1ff.).

THE BASIS OF SUBMISSION

Paul appeals to three motivations in his emphasis on the necessity (*dio anagkē*) for submission (v. 5). First, there is the ordinance of God (*diatagē Theou*) to this effect.[45] Civil disobedience makes one a rebel against the order (*taxis*) of God.

Second, there is fear (*phobos*) of wrath (*orgē*) and judgment (*krisis*),[46] according to verse 2. It is likely that the KJV rendering "damnation" is an unnecessary

[44]See Strack and Billerbeck, *Kommentar*, 3:305, for examples.

[45]*Diatagē* occurs in the New Testament only here and in Acts 7:53. We have earlier called attention to the piling up of words from *tassein* in the passage.

[46]F. Büchsel, "*Krisis*," *TDNT*, 3:941f.

strengthening of the idea the apostle expresses. Though one may debate the matter, it is more likely that the adverse verdict of the magistrate is the matter primarily in view.[47] The same ambiguity resides in "wrath" (*orgē*).[48] But it is more likely that the apostle has in view that the evildoer may expect to face the wrath of the magistrate whose right it is to wield the sword,[49] which, as we have earlier said, is a penal judgment of God.

Third, there is conscience (*suneidēsis*). *Dia tēn suneidēsin* means the Christian's own conscience which is bound by the Lord's command. The phrase is comparable to *dia ton kurion* (cf. 1 Pet. 2:13, 19). By disobedience, one would incur a guilty conscience. The Christian strives for a conscience void of offense toward God and men (Acts 24:16). He might also by his action wound the conscience of a brother (cf. 1 Cor. 8:10). The Christian fulfills his duty because he has a knowledge of the relation in which the magistrate stands to God.[50]

[47]Eventually, of course, God's judgment is to be faced. There are ample New Testament examples of *krisis* for God's judgment: Mk. 12:40; Jas. 3:1. John Calvin, *Commentaries on the Epistle of Paul the Apostle to the Romans,* trans. John Owen (reprint ed., Grand Rapids, Mich.: Wm. B. Eerdmans Publishing Co., 1979), p. 479, aptly remarked, "And by judgment, I understand not only the punishment which is inflicted by the magistrate, as though he had only said, that they would be justly punished who resisted authority, but also the vengeance of God, however it may at length be executed: For he teacheth us in general what end awaits those who contend with God."

[48]*Orgē* is used twelve times in Romans. It often is the wrath of God as in Eph. 4:32; see G. Stählin, "*Orgē,*" *TDNT*, 5:441f.

[49]*Eikē* is also in 1 Cor. 15:2; Gal. 3:4; cf. F. Büchsel, "*Eikē,*" *TDNT*, 2:477-78.

[50]Cranfield, "Observations," pp. 246-47; see also the study of C. A. Pierce, *Conscience in the New Testament* (London: SCM Press, 1955).

WHAT IF?

Though the question next raised lies outside the topic discussed in this pericope by the apostle, and is therefore outside this specific discussion, in the light of history one can hardly avoid raising it. When the demand of the magistrate is not prayer, tax, tribute, reverence, and honor, but is that which conscience cannot render, what is to be done? To this confrontation, only one choice remains: "We must obey God rather than men" (Acts 5:29). And for such an answer there is undoubtedly a price to be paid:

> If any one is to be taken captive, to captivity he goes; if any one slays with the sword, with the sword must he be slain. Here is a call for the endurance and faith of the saints (Rev. 13:10, Codex A).

11

Servants or Deaconesses?

Romans 16:1

In my opinion, the question of female appointees in the early church turns upon the interpretation given to two New Testament passages, both of which are indecisive, and in turn the interpretation given them has to be examined in the light of the history of the early church.

Phoebe was a *diakonos* of the church in Cenchrea (Rom. 16:1); but one is immediately confronted with definition problems. Was she an appointee of that congregation or merely one of the thousands of females through history who have served the church? *Diakonos* is an indeclinable Greek word which occurs many times in the New Testament (Mt. 20:26; 22:13; 23:11; Mk. 9:35;

10:43; Jn. 2:5; 12:26; Rom. 13:4; 15:8; 16:1; 1 Cor. 3:5; 2 Cor. 3:6; 6:4; 11:15, 23; Gal. 2:17; Eph. 3:7; 4:7; 6:21; Phil. 1:1; Col. 1:7, 23, 25; 1 Thess. 3:2; 1 Tim. 3:8, 12; 4:6). "Servant" or "minister" would be the most likely rendering of this term; however, the KJV transliterated it in three instances, thereby perpetuating or creating a religious jargon for organization of the church. Even in Phil. 1:1 and 1 Tim. 3:8, 12, "minister" might well be more what the Lord had in mind and would safeguard us from the trap of appointing men who are given nothing to do and who do not conceive of their position as implying that they are to serve. Alexander Campbell thought that high churchmanship had caused the KJV translators to perpetuate the organization they knew by this translating procedure.

In the case of Phoebe, who is the only female in the New Testament to whom *diakonos* is applied, Tyndale (1525) used "minister"; and that term was used in the Great Bible (1539), the Bishops' Bible (1568), and the Rheims (1582). It was the Geneva Bible (1560) which contributed "servant," and it was followed by the KJV (1611), the ASV (1901), the NIV (1973), and the NKJV (1979). The RSV (1946) made the innovation for the English Bible by transliterating the term as "deaconess," and the NIV gave this reading as a marginal option. Translations do not determine the meaning of New Testament passages; they merely reflect the understanding of translating groups. In view of the nontechnical use of *diakonos* in many New Testament passages, no man can say on the basis of New Testament material alone whether Phoebe was merely a servant or was an appointee.

Equally ambiguous on the question is the second New Testament passage where, in qualification lists (1 Tim.

3:11), we read "even so *must their wives be* grave . . . " (KJV; emphasis mine). This passage stood as "wives" in English translations from the time of Tyndale until the RV/ASV (1981, 1901) except for the Rheims which had "the women." The RV/ASV take up "women" and in that they are followed by the RSV. The NIV gives "wives" in the text, but has "deaconesses" as a marginal option. The English translations reflect the inbuilt obscurity that there is in the Greek word *gunē*. As in rural America, "woman" may describe either a female or a wife—a man may say "that is my woman"—so *gunē* may describe a female or a wife. Which is implied must come from the context; but the context in 1 Tim. 3:11 is not dogmatically clear as the above cited variants in the English translations reflect. One interprets the passage in keeping with presuppositions he holds. If he thinks the early church had female appointees, then he understands the list to be talking of deaconesses. If he thinks that it did not, then he takes the term and its qualifications to be describing the wives of the deacons. On the basis of the New Testament text alone, neither side of the debate is likely going to persuade the other. *Gunē* occurs many times in the New Testament, and in the letter to Timothy has the meaning of "female" in 1 Tim. 2:9-12, 14. But it also has the meaning of "wife" in 1 Tim. 3:2, 12; 5:9.

There is not much way to make progress in the discussion but to have recourse to church history to see what the situation was in the early church. In the documents of the early church, there were in the congregations elders and deacons, and after the time of Ignatius there was the monarchial bishop; but there is very little evidence for female appointees in the second and early third centuries. Before Ignatius, presbyter (*presbuteros*) and bishop (*episcopos*) were used interchangeably; but after that time a pyramid organization with the bishop at the top and under him elders and deacons is to be seen.

The one item in this period relevant to women's position in the organization is Pliny's letter to the Emperor Trajan. This correspondence, dealing with how Pliny treated Christians in Bithynia about A.D. 110, is in Latin.

> I judge it so much the more necessary to extract the real truth, with the assistance of torture, from two female slaves, who were styled deaconesses; but I could discover nothing more than depraved and excessive superstition.[1]

The Latin term is *quae ministrae dicebantur*; however, *ministrae* has within it the same obscurity that *diakonos* has with which we started. They could be servants of the church, or they could be appointees of the church. No one can know. However, in light of the fact that Christian sources of this century do not mention such female appointees though they do discuss church organization, the person who wants to make them appointees needs to prove his case. He cannot do that.

When we come to the third-century church orders, the situation is entirely different. By that time, the church does have female appointees in its organization. The Syrian *Didascalia* of the late third century has deaconesses who assist at the baptism of women, go into the houses of heathen where there are believing women, visit the sick, minister to them, and bathe them.[2] Shepherd in *The Interpreter's Dictionary of the Bible* says, "Our chief sources about the order of deaconesses derive from the

[1]Pliny *Epistle* 10.97.

[2]*Didascalia Apostolorum*, trans. R. Hugh Connolly (Oxford, England: Clarendon Press, 1929), pp. 146-48.

Church Orders and conciliar decrees of the fourth-fifth centuries. The order does not appear to have been in existence in the church of Rome."[3]

In light of this evidence, I think the drive to have deaconesses (in the appointee sense) in the church is very hard-put to prove that it has New Testament authority.

A further significant contribution to the on-going discussion might be made if one noticed that when deaconesses did appear in the church organization, they kept the doors, aided in female baptisms, and did other work with women. The modern drive for deaconesses would not be at all satisfied with doing such tasks.

[3]Massey H. Shepherd, Jr., "Deaconess," in *The Interpreter's Dictionary of the Bible*, ed. George Arthur Buttrick (New York: Abingdon Press, 1962), 1:786-87.

12

"Mark Them Which Cause Divisions"

Romans 16:17

The obligation, almost universally felt among our preaching brothers, to label other preaching brothers who hold positions thought to be erroneous, rests upon a misunderstanding of Rom. 16:17 which in the KJV and the ASV reads:

> Now I beseech you, brethren, mark them which cause divisions and offenses contrary to the doctrine which ye have learned; and avoid them.

Under the influence of the KJV and the ASV, we have men who apparently feel their chief mission in life is the branding in the eyes of the whole church all those who differ with them. We have a type of journalism whose chief function seems to be to attack the reputation of those who differ with the views of the editors and writers for those journals. How often we have heard a man defend his attack by saying, "The Bible says, 'Mark those which cause divisions,' and so I am marking him!" The man then proceeds with his attack, fully confident that he is righteous and is doing the will of God. It seems to me that the branders might well contemplate the words of F. F. Bruce:

> When a man's standing in the constituency which he serves, not to mention his livelihood, depends on his reputation for fidelity to the truth of Scripture, it is a very serious matter for anyone else to broadcast doubts about his fidelity or orthodoxy. If he himself statedly renounces something which is the essence of the historic Christian faith, he will be prepared for the consequences, but he should not be held responsible for the inferences which other people may draw from his statements. Most deplorable of all is the launching of a whispering campaign to the effect that so and so is "going off the rails" or is "getting far from the Lord."[1]

The Greek word which is used in Rom. 16:17 is *skopein* which in classical sources means "to look at" and especially "to look at critically." In the New Testament, it has meaning in one passage "to consider something critically and then to hold something before one as a model on the basis of the inspection" (Phil. 3:17).[2] Other interesting occurrences of this verb include: "Take heed therefore that the light which is in thee be not darkness" (Lk. 11:35); "we look not at the things which are seen, but at

[1]F. F. Bruce, *In Retrospect* (Grand Rapids, Mich.: Wm. B. Eerdmans Publishing Co., 1980), pp. 188-89.

[2]Ernst Fuchs, "*Skopein*," *TDNT*, 3:414-16.

the things which are not seen . . ." (2 Cor. 4:18); ". . . considering thyself, lest thou also be tempted" (Gal. 6:1); and "Look not every man on his own things, but every man also on the things of others" (Phil. 2:4).

It can be seen that the KJV rendered *skopein*, which never has the connotation of "to brand," in other passages with "take heed" (ASV: look; Lk. 11:35); "mark" (Rom. 16:17; Phil. 3:17); "look" (2 Cor. 4:18; Phil. 2:4); and "consider" (ASV: looking; Gal. 6:1). *Skopein* is the root from which *episkopein* which is rendered "looking diligently" (ASV: looking carefully; Heb. 12:13) and "exercise the oversight" (1 Pet. 5:2) comes. This last case describes the function of the elders (*episkopoi*; Acts 20:28; Phil. 1:1; 1 Tim. 1:7; 3:2; 1 Pet. 2:25) of the church. Also the word *episcope* (visitation; Lk. 19:44); "bishoprick" [*sic*] (ASV: office; Acts 1:20) and "office of a bishop" (1 Tim. 3:1) comes from this root.

What has happened is that men confident that they understand their version of Scripture have misunderstood it. The verb "mark" occurs three times in the KJV and the ASV New Testament. The other occurrences are not at all taken by the ordinary reader in the sense of branding. One verse says: "He marked how they chose out the chief rooms" (ASV: seats; Lk. 14:7). That the meaning is "He observed" can be grasped by all. The second case says: "Brethren, be followers together of me, and mark them which walk so as ye have us for an example" (Phil. 3:17, KJV). Here again the meaning is "to take notice of."

The verb "mark" in the KJV Old Testament has the meaning "to understand" (rendering *bin*; Job 18:2); "to seal" or "shut up" (*chatham*; Job 24:16); "to know" (*yada'*; Ruth 3:4; 1 Kings 20:7, 22); "to face front" (*panah*; Job 21:5); "to give attention" (*qashabh*; Jer. 23:18); "to see" (*ra'ah*); and "to observe" or "watch" (*shamar*; 1 Sam. 1:12; Job 10:14; 22:15; 31:11; 39:1; Ps. 37:37; 56:6; 139:3). The phrase "mark well" renders *qashabh* meaning "to give attention" (Job 33:31) and *sim lebh* meaning "to set the heart on" (Ps. 48:13; Ezek. 44:5). None of these cases are of "branding" import.

The verb "mark" in 1611 meant "to take notice of"; it carried no connotation of branding. It did not suggest that one should do what the Lord did when he put a mark on Cain. It did not propose that an "A" should be put on the breast of the adulterer as was done in Hawthorne's *The Scarlet Letter*. Today, apart from the phrase "mark my word," "mark" is seldom used in the sense of "take notice of" but does primarily carry the sense that it is most commonly understood by our people when they read Rom. 16:17. They register the meaning they know best, not asking themselves if that is the correct one.

A glance at the translations made in the last forty years reveals that they all, without exception, set forth clearly the import of *skopein* in Rom. 16:17. They read, "take note of" (RSV); "keep an eye on" (NASV; NEB); "note" (NKJV); "watch out for" (TEV; NIV); and "stay away from" (TLB). The difference between "watch out for" and "brand" is comparable to that which exists between the actions of legal law enforcement personnel and those of vigilantes.

My concern is not against exercising discipline in the church, for discipline is a duty put upon us by God. It is not against contending earnestly for the faith. It is not against safeguarding the flock from grievous wolves. It is not against vigilance, but only against vigilantes. My concern is only against proof-texting which attaches meanings to words that they did not have when a translation was made, and which are meanings that cannot be supported by the original language in which God gave his revelation. It appears that some have made a whole rule of ethics out of a meaning a word should not carry at all in the context of the New Testament in which it is used.

With the shift that has come in meaning of words since 1611, one can easily misunderstand that which he is confident he understands.

13

"Spiritual Words" or "Spiritual Men"?

1 Corinthians 2:13

Paul claimed the direction of the Holy Spirit in his teaching. To possible recalcitrants in Corinth, he said:

> If any one thinks that he is a prophet, or spiritual, he should acknowledge that what I am writing to you is a command of the Lord (1 Cor. 14:37).

He commended the Thessalonians:

> When you received the word of God which you heard from us, you accepted it not as the word of men but as what it really is, the word of God, which is at work in you believers (1 Thess. 2:13).

The question that needs to be considered in 1 Cor. 2:13

does not challenge that guidance, for Paul plainly claims it:

> And we impart this in words not taught by human wisdom but taught by the Spirit, interpreting spiritual truths to those who possess the Spirit.

The first part of this passage, which is a suitable reply to the sneer about the quality of Paul's speech found in 2 Cor. 10:10, is not obscure, and its import is not at the center of our consideration at this time. It is the final clause, which in Greek is *pneumatikois pneumatika sugkrinontes*, that raises an issue.

The verb *sugkrinein* is also used by Paul in 2 Cor. 10:12 where it clearly means "compare"; and some English versions have used this meaning in 1 Cor. 2:13. However, *sugkrinein* in the Septuagint has the meaning of "interpret," especially of dreams (Gen. 40:8, 16, 22; 45:12, 15; Judg. 7:15; Dan. 5:12, 15-16), and that meaning is chosen by other English versions for 1 Cor. 2:13. It is argued that this context is not a comparing context. *Sugkrinontes* is a participial form qualifying *laloumen* (speaking) which is in the first clause of the verse. The object of this participle is *pneumatika* (spiritual things), a neuter plural form. *Pneumatikois*, the other word of the phrase, can be either a neuter plural or a masculine plural dative form; and that sets the interpretive problem of the verse.

Pneumatikos (spiritual) occurs in New Testament passages describing a wide range of inanimate and animate objects. The law (Rom. 7:14), the gifts in the early church (Rom. 1:11; 15:27; 1 Cor. 9:11), food and drink in the wilderness (1 Cor. 10:3), miraculous gifts (1 Cor. 12:1; 14:1), the heavenly body yet to be received (1 Cor. 15:44), the Christian's blessings in Christ (Eph. 1:3), his songs (Eph. 5:19; Col. 3:16), the hosts of wickedness (Eph. 6:12), and the Christian's sacrifices (1 Pet. 2:5), are all spiritual. In contrast, when the word is used for persons, it designates those who possessed gifts in the early church (1 Cor. 14:37) and the Christian who has made progress in the Christian life (1 Cor. 2:15; 3:1; Gal. 6:1). Within itself, *pneumatikos* could designate either things or persons in 1 Cor. 2:13.

In the immediate context of 1 Cor. 2:13, an adverb *pneumatikōs* from the same Greek root lies back of the phrase "spiritually discerned" (1 Cor. 2:14). This adverb also occurs in Rev. 11:8 (spiritually called). But Paul in the context in 1 Corinthians 2 contrasts the unspiritual man *psuchikos* with spiritual (*pneumatikos*). He says, "the spiritual man [*pneumatikos*] judges all things, but is himself to be judged by no one" (1 Cor. 2:15). He then chides the Corinthians for not being "spiritual" (1 Cor. 3:1). Paul's discussion of the spiritual man lies at the heart of the contention that *pneumatikos* in 1 Cor. 2:13 also speaks of persons rather than of things. Taken in this way, one then is carried back in thought to "the mature" (*en tois teleiois*) of 1 Cor. 2:6.

Pneumatikos in Greek is in the dative case. The dative has two well known uses: one expresses the instrument; the other expresses the indirect object. With the forms for the two uses exactly alike, there is no infallible way to know in which category a dative falls. Interpreters usually depend on the context for guidance. In 1 Cor. 2:13, the context does not make a clear distinction possible. Furthermore, the masculine and neuter forms in the dative plural are identical in Greek, making it uncertain which gender the writer intended. Also, one must decide whether he is to take the context from that which goes before or that which follows the clause. Some interpreters go back to *didaktois logois* (words . . .

taught) and consider that the *pneumatikois* should be "spiritual words," the instrument of the discerning. However, it is less than certain that *pneumatikois* (spiritual) modifies an unstated noun (*logois*); the commentaries list numerous other possibilities prepared by those who contend that we are dealing with a neuter concept. Others contend for an indirect object, consider as persuasive the context mentioned in the above paragraph, and find the teaching spoken of to be given to "spiritual men."

This long-standing dispute can be seen in the variety reflected in English translations. The Vulgate rendered 1 Cor. 2:13 as *spiritualibus spiritualia conparantes.* William Tyndale (1525), translator of the first English printed New Testament, followed the Latin: "making spretuall [*sic*] comparisons to spretuall [*sic*] things." This rendering was continued in the Great Bible (1539), but the Geneva Bible (1560) had "comparing spiritual things with spiritual things." The Rheims Bible (1582) modified this rendering to "comparing spiritual things to spiritual," and the KJV (1611) differed from the rendering only by substituting the preposition "with" for "to" as the Geneva had: "comparing spiritual things with spiritual."

The RV (1881) and ASV (1901) further modified the rendering to "combining spiritual things with spiritual *words*," but carried the marginal alternative: "or 'interpreting spiritual things to spiritual men.' "

The twentieth-century translations divide over the interpretation along the lines we have outlined above. Following an interpretation possibility already used by John Wycliffe ("makien [*sic*] a likeness of spiyritual [*sic*] things to goostli [*sic*] men"), the RSV took the relevant phrase as an indirect object: "spiritual things to those who possess the Spirit," but offers two alternates in the footnotes: "Or 'interpreting spiritual truths in spiritual language; or comparing spiritual things with spiritual.'" The NEB has: "We are interpreting spiritual truths to those who have the Spirit"; the TEV has: "We explain spiritual truths to those who have the Spirit," but has marginal options: "to those who have the Spirit; or with words given by the Spirit"; and William Barclay has: "When we interpret spiritual truths to people that have the Spirit. . . ."

On the other side of the issue, Ronald Knox had "matching what is spiritual with what is spiritual"; the NASV chose "combining spiritual *thoughts* with spiritual *words*"; and TLB had: "So we use the Holy Spirit's words to explain the Holy Spirit's facts," and gives marginal option, "Or, 'interpreting spiritual truths in spiritual language.'" The NIV gives: "expressing spiritual truths in spiritual words," and has a footnote option "interpreting spiritual truths to spiritual men"; the NAB has: "interpreting spiritual things in spiritual terms"; the Simple English Bible has: "We explain scriptural things with spiritual words"; and, finally, the NKJV continues the KJV rendering "comparing spiritual things with spiritual."

These many cases have not been cited to suggest that counting noses solves anything in biblical study. They show the complexity of the problem, the uncertainty of the interpretation, and the interpretative freedom which translators have exercised.

A friend of mine came back from a translating conference reporting that those he had been advising had subscribed to a whole theology built on the italicized words in the traditional translations. They had ignored that the words their thought was depending upon had been supplied by the translators and were not in the

Greek text at all. I, myself, have heard internationally known figures cite 1 Cor. 2:13 in the ASV form as a proof text with major emphasis on the final use of "words"—"spiritual *words*"—as though this were the clear major intent of the verse.

In the Old Testament, people listened to the false prophets because those prophets were saying the things they wanted to hear; they rejected the messages of men like Amos, Jeremiah, and Ezekiel because they were saying what they did not want to hear. The Lord threatens:

> Any man of the house of Israel who takes his idols into his heart and sets the stumbling block of his iniquity before his face, and yet comes to the prophet, I the Lord will answer him myself because of the multitude of his idols (Ezek. 14:4).

To take an obscure passage of Scripture where two interpretations are both equally possible, to interpret it in a way congenial to one's thought, and after that to support that thought by the interpretation which has been chosen is not only circular reasoning, it is a subtle form of self-deception. It is a form of the same sort of trap those Old Testament people fell into. No proposition can be more certain than the evidence upon which it rests. Until we are able to solve the problems created by the context, the gender, and the usage of the dative case, we should keep the interpretation of the final clause of 1 Cor. 2:13 in the category of the uncertain. My intent is not to discuss the idea of inspiration, but merely to call attention to a problem in proof-texting.

14

Remarriage
1 Corinthians 7

In 1 Corinthians 7 Paul discusses questions about which the Corinthians had written him. Unfortunately, we do not have their letter and we have to deduce from between the lines what their questions were. Any exchange looked at from only one side is never completely seen.

Paul points out that the rights and obligations of marriage are mutual, not to be denied by either party of a marriage. He prefers that the single not marry, but concedes that marriage for them is preferable over their being tormented with passion (vv. 1-7).

The wife is not to separate from her husband, and if

she does she has two options—one is to remain single and the other is to be reconciled to her husband. The husband should not divorce his wife (vv. 10-11).

The Christian married to an unbeliever who is willing to continue the marriage is not to divorce the unbeliever. Arguing from a premise that he and the Corinthians jointly held, Paul asserts that the children of such a marriage are holy; hence, the unbeliever in such a marriage is consecrated through the believer. Paul is not asserting that the marriage saves such a person, but that the marriage is a genuine marriage from which the unbeliever may be brought to salvation (vv. 12-16). If the unbeliever wishes to separate, the brother or sister is not bound, "for God has called us to peace." Paul here seems to grant that separation is preferable to continuous fighting with an unbeliever who wants out of the marriage (v. 15).

Paul proceeds to say that he would have people stay in the condition in which they were called to the Christian life—whether married or single (vv. 17-24). He speaks of an impending distress (without defining it) which makes it preferable for the single to remain single. He describes it as an approaching condition of society in which marriages would be disrupted, as would be mourning, rejoicing, and commerce (vv. 25-31). In such a time, whereas the wife or husband has to worry about the welfare of the partner, the single has only his own well-being to consider and, therefore, can devote himself with single-mindedness to the service of God. Though Paul does not elaborate on the conditions, one can see that if a time of persecution came, the married person would have to consider that his death for his faith would leave his wife alone. The single person would have no such burden to entice him to deny the faith. His ties with this world are less.

Paul's statements in verses 36 through 38 will always be perplexing. The translators of the KJV seem to have envisioned the section as dealing with a father's treatment of his daughter. The ASV made this interpretation clear in italics. However, neither translation gave us a clear insight into what "he behaveth himself uncomely toward his virgin" must mean. The twentieth century translations tend to interpret the passage as discussing a man and the woman he is in love with rather than father and daughter. Leaving our perplexities aside, though Paul prefers the single state, he grants that the man who marries the woman does well.

Finally, Paul affirms that marriage is for life—a woman is bound to her husband as long as he lives; but if he is dead, she can marry whomever she wishes "only in the Lord." Even here Paul would prefer that she remain unmarried (vv. 39-40).

The things that Paul did not say bother us now more than the things that he did say. In particular, we puzzle over "the brother or sister is not bound" (v. 15). It is easy to understand that Paul is saying they are not bound to continue in a marriage with an unbeliever when the unbeliever is not willing to go on. But the question we want to ask is, "What then?"

Paul used the Greek verb *dedoulōtai* (v. 15) which occurs in eight New Testament passages: Egyptians enslaved the Israelites (Acts 7:6); Christians in conversion become slaves of righteousness (Rom. 6:18); they become slaves of God (Rom. 6:22); Paul made himself a slave of all (1 Cor. 9:19); before conversion Christians were slaves to the elemental spirits of the universe (Gal. 4:3); older women are not to be slaves to drink (Tit. 2:3); and troublemakers in the church are slaves of corruption (2 Pet. 2:19). While these cases give insight into the meaning of *douloun* in the New Testament, they do not make any contribution to our question: "What next after the divorce?"

First Cor. 7:15 came into English with John Wycliffe in the form: "For whi the brother or sistir is not suget to seruage in siche"; and into printed English with William Tyndale as "a brother or sister is not in subjection to soche." With the Geneva Bible, it became "in subjection in suche things"; in the Bishops' Bible as "is not made subject in such *things*"; and in the Rheims as "is not subject to servitude in such." With the KJV (and later the ASV), it became "is not under bondage in such cases"; the Smith-Goodspeed had "In such cases the brother or sister is not a slave"; and then with the RSV it became "in such a case the brother or sister is not bound." The twentieth-century translations have not made essential improvements: NASV, NAB, NKJV read "not under bondage in such cases"; the NIV, "not bound in such circumstances"; the TEV, "in such cases the Christian partner . . . is free to act"; and TLB, "the Christian . . . should not insist that the other stay." All of these make clear that the Christian is a free person; none of them make any contribution to the question, "What next?"

With these obscurities, some say that the person divorced by the unbeliever is free to marry someone else, as 80 percent of the divorced for whatever reason in the United States now do in the first three years after divorce. Others say, "Not so." In my opinion there is a quite simple reason for our translations not making the matter clear, as well as for our inability to be able to convince each other of our respective positions. We are asking the passage a question that Paul was not discussing! As a general rule (if not a comprehensive one) when one asks a biblical passage a question that the writer was not answering, he obtains from it the answer he has either consciously or unconsciously accepted on some other basis. He merely uses the passage to support a position he already occupies. It confirms him in his belief, but he cannot convince others with it.

The theologians who went before us taught us that biblical authority is found in direct command (or prohibition), approved example, and necessary inference. Those who resort to logic on 1 Cor. 7:15 wish to argue that "is not bound" must mean "is free to marry someone else." Their logic is an inference, but not a necessary one. The person has three options—to remain single, to be reconciled to the divorced one, or to be married to someone else. The third option is not a necessary inference from the passage.

For these reasons, it would seem to me that 1 Cor. 7:15 is no reason to supplement the Gospel with its "except fornication" (Mt. 5:32; 19:9) with an additional cause for remarriage—"previous marriage to an unbeliever" who wanted out of the marriage.

15

"Virgin *Daughter*"

1 Corinthians 7:36-38

> If any one thinks that he is not behaving properly toward his betrothed, if his passions are strong, and it has to be, let him do as he wishes: let them marry—it is no sin. But whoever is firmly established in his heart, being under no necessity but having his desire under control, and has determined this in his heart, to keep her as his betrothed, he will do well. So that he who marries his betrothed does well; and he who refrains from marriage will do better (1 Cor. 7:36-38).

In his list of objections to the renderings of the TEV, A. G. Hobbs includes 1 Cor. 7:36-38. The issues in the interpretation of these verses are issues of long standing.

The first issue of the passage concerns the phrase "virgin *daughter*" with "daughter" in italics and with "virgin" as an alternative rendering in the margin of the ASV. Earlier English Bibles from the time of William Tyndale had been content with "virgin" in the text. The ASV translators of the passage make clear that they understand the masculine pronoun to have an understood "father" as the antecedent of "his" throughout the passage.

However, having made this assumption, they do not at all make clear how the father "behaveth himself unseemly toward his virgin *daughter*," and we must ask what this phrase means. Have we a problem of incest? Have we a case of a father's denying marriage to the girl? Neither do the ASV translators clarify the phrase "let them marry," where the pronoun in their rendering stands without any antecedent at all. Surely one can see that someone could ask the absurd question, "Are the father and virgin daughter to marry?" Grammatically, though not logically, the two would form the most normal antecedent of "them."

Long before the ASV, the English Bible had laid the foundation for the interpretation the ASV used. Tyndale and his successors translated verse 38, "He that joineth his virgin in marriage doeth well," leaving the reader to figure out for himself who the antecedent of "he" is, and it seems to me that it could conceivably be the lover. But the Geneva Bible read, "he that giveth in marriage." Except for the Rheims Bible which uses "joineth in marriage," "giveth" maintains itself in the English Bible from the Geneva Bible until the RSV. The KJV merely substitutes the pronoun "her" as the Geneva Bible had done for "his own virgin," giving us "He that giveth *her* in marriage," removing all doubt that the father is intended to be understood as the antecedent. The ASV moved further to eliminate the obscurity by inserting "daughter" while being more literal with "his own virgin *daughter*."

It is openly admitted by the current commentaries that we do not know what the verses mean. The difficulties—beyond that of the antecedent which we have just described—turn on two words. The first is the well known Greek word *parthenos*, which means "virgin" and ordinarily is not obscure. It occurs in the New Testament twelve times and designates unmarried women (Mt. 1:23; Lk. 1:27; 25:1; Acts 21:9; 1 Cor. 7:25, 28, 34, 36-38) except in two figurative uses, one in 2 Cor. 11:2 and the other in Rev. 14:4 where it designates Christians as pure individuals. While *parthenos* could readily designate unmarried daughters, ordinarily it would not primarily be used to designate the father-daughter relationship. Furthermore, the individualized possessive, "his own virgin," creates some problems should one envision a family of a father with several daughters. There seems little justification for supplying "daughter" in italics in this passage.

The second issue centers on the word *gamizō* which is in verse 38, as contrasted with *gameō* of verse 36. There is a textual variant on the passage, and the *Textus Receptus* has *ekgamizō*, which means to give in marriage. Greek writer Apollonius states that the distinction between these two verbs which occur in our verse is that men marry and the women are given in marriage. *Gamizein* is otherwise found only in Christian writings so that Apollonius' statement cannot be checked in secular Greek usage.

Gamizein occurs in the New Testament in the statement, "For in the resurrection they neither marry nor are given in marriage" (Mt. 22:30; Mk. 12:25; Lk. 20:35), and in the statement that in the days of Noah "they were marrying and giving in marriage" (Mt. 24:38; Lk. 17:27). Each of these statements has the same two verbs, *gameō* and *gamizō*, which are in 1 Corinthians 7, and they would appear to support the contention that a distinction is to be made between them.

However, it is asserted by Moulton-Milligan that there are cases where *izō* verbs took on the meaning of *eō* verbs and that our passage may be such a case. Assuming that this has happened, then the passage talks of a man marrying his virgin, that is, the girl with whom he is in love, and not of a father marrying off his daughter. The RSV took the passage this way and envisioned that a man's fiancée is designated by the word *parthenos* and proceeds to render *parthenos* as "betrothed"—quite a case of interpretation on their part! Others have envisioned that in the church in Corinth there were spiritual marriages—that is, cases where men and women lived together under a pledge of celibacy to each other. Paul is then saying that if the temptation to marriage becomes too strong, there is no sin in making their marriage a real marriage.

These are the issues of this passage. The proposed solutions remain hypothetical. I think we have pursued the topic as far as we can.

16

"Without Discerning The Body"

1 Corinthians 11:29

In attempting to determine the meaning of the phrase "without discerning the body" (1 Cor. 11:29), which Paul uses as a blameworthy fault in his discussion of the Lord's Supper in 1 Corinthians, one must first look at the verb used. How is "discern" to be understood? The verb *diakrinein* occurs in the New Testament as a verb in the active voice in eight passages (Mt. 16:3; Acts 11:12; 15:9; 1 Cor. 4:7; 6:5; 11:29, 31; 14:29) and occurs in the passive voice in nine passages and in one Gospel parallel (Mt. 21:21; Mk. 11:23; Acts 10:20; 11:2; Rom. 4:20; 14:23; Jas. 1:6 [twice]; 2:4; Jude 9, 22). The verb *diakrinein* in the active voice means to make a distinction or to differentiate,[1] but it carries no innate suggestion about what is being distinguished between. The person in Corinth who does not distinguish between common bread and fruit of the vine and the bread and the cup in the Lord's Supper would not be discerning the body (of the Lord); but it can also be argued that the person not recognizing his congregational obligations and relationships is not discerning the body (i.e., the church).

The noun *diakrisis*, derived from the verb, usually means "differentiation"; it is used for differentiation between spirits (1 Cor. 12:10) and between good and evil (Heb. 5:14), and is also back of the expression "not for disputes over opinions" (Rom. 14:1), where it means "evaluations."[2] One cannot decide from the study of either the verb or the noun what is being distinguished between in 1 Cor. 11:29. The Kittel dictionary defines the passage as, "because he does not distinguish the body of the Lord (from ordinary bread)."[3] What is the validity of this opinion?

Next, notice that 1 Cor. 11:29 has a textual variant with the Byzantine text (translated in the KJV and NKJV) reading, "the Lord's body" (*to sōma tou kuriou*), and the shorter text (given in the Nestle and the Bible Societies' Greek text and followed in the RSV and NIV) reading merely, "the body" (*to sōma*). The shorter reading gets only a "C" probability rating in the Textual Commentary. The editors state that they cannot easily explain how *tou kuriou* could have been dropped out were it original.[4] Although "the Lord's body" could be

[1]Bauer, *Greek-English Lexicon*, p. 185.

[2]Friedrich Büchsel, "*Diakrisis*," *TDNT*, 3:949-50.

[3]Friedrich Büchsel, "*Diakrinō*," *TDNT*, 3:946.

[4]Bruce M. Metzger, *A Textual Commentary on the Greek New Testament* (London/New York: United Bible Societies, 1971), pp. 562-63.

understood as "the church," it is hardly to be questioned that the Byzantine authorities understood it as the crucified body of Jesus, which fits the near context of this passage.

When one turns to consider the body that is being discerned, he notices that "body" (*to sōma*) occurs three times in close proximity in Paul's discussion of the Lord's Supper (1 Cor. 11:24-29). After blessing and breaking the bread, Jesus said, "This is my body which is for you" (v. 24). The Byzantine text followed in the KJV and NKJV adds "which is broken," giving the reading as "my body which is broken for you." No person would think of arguing that this verse is speaking of the church as the body of Christ. It speaks of the Lord's incarnate body which went to the cross. The statement contains a metaphor in which one thing is said to be another because it resembles it in some way. The use of "body" here is not different from its use in the three synoptic Gospels (Mt. 26:26; Mk. 14:22; Lk. 22:19).

Verse 27 points out that "whoever eats the bread or the cup of the Lord in an unworthy manner will be guilty of profaning [*enochos estai*] the body and blood of the Lord." Again, no thinking person would suppose that it is the church which is to be eaten or to be profaned. The contrast between body and blood make such an understanding completely impossible. The church was purchased with the Lord's blood (Acts 20:28), but no passage speaks of the church as being the Lord's blood. The apostle is still speaking of the Lord's personal body and blood. The offender is guilty of profaning that which the bread and the cup represent.

Verse 28 continues the same topic by admonishing a man to examine himself and so eat of the bread and drink of the cup. The topic has not changed. The same two items of the preceding verse are continued. The next verse has the third occurrence of "body" in this context: "For any one who eats and drinks [the same actions] without discerning the body eats and drinks judgment upon himself" (v. 29). Has the meaning of body here changed without any hint being given? What is the meaning of "the body" which is spoken of?

According to a popular interpretation, we are supposed to think that Paul has suddenly shifted gears after using "body" twice in the context in a perfectly clear sense to using it here not of the actual body of Jesus, but of the church as the body of Christ. That is, the person who is taking the Lord's Supper without properly recognizing the community as the body of Christ is the guilty one.

For Paul to have chosen words in such an arbitrary and cryptic way without giving any hint that he is doing so is indeed a strange use of language. The Corinthian correspondence does know the church as the body of Christ (1 Cor. 12:12ff.)—as do the Roman (Rom. 12:4), Ephesian (Eph. 4:12ff.), and Colossian (Col. 3:15) letters—but that fact does not establish a shift of vocabulary in 1 Cor. 11:29. Usually when Paul uses "body" for the church, the meaning is obvious and is not to be confused with the Lord's incarnate body or his heavenly body.

Paul is quite explicit that the Lord's Supper has fellowship connotations. "The bread which we break, is it not a participation in the body of Christ? Because there is one bread, we who are many are one body, for we all partake of the one bread" (1 Cor. 10:16-17). The fact that Paul in the preceding statement speaks of participation in the blood of Christ makes it impossible that "the body of Christ" in which we participate in this verse is the church, though "the one body" mentioned is. There is, however, no mystery. The shift in definition of "body" is completely clear. One does not have to be told that "body of Christ" and "one body" are two different things in this setting.

One readily recognizes that one of the problems of observing the Lord's Supper in Corinth was that there were divisions among the people (1 Cor. 11:18). The Sermon on the Mount makes clear the need to be reconciled to one's brother when one goes to worship (Mt. 5:23-24). The sharing together in the act is a significant part of the Lord's Supper.

None of these considerations, however, seems to establish the case that Paul used "body" (*sōma*) in two different senses in 1 Cor. 11:24-29. That he did is merely a possibility and not a very likely one at that. I would like to see a detailed demonstration to the contrary rather than just dogmatic assertions that he did.

Though counting noses does not settle any problem, the alignment of the commentaries is at least interesting. On the one side, Neville Clark said,

> Because the body has a double reference and Christ and his church are organically one, to fail to discern the body was to be guilty of profaning the body and the blood of the Lord; to indulge in gross misconduct at the supper and to violate the fellowship of the Church's common life was one and the same sin meriting one and the same condemnation.[5]

Carl Holladay said,

> . . . the entire context suggests that the phrase also, if not exclusively, implies "discerning the body, the church" (cf. 12:12ff.). Observance of the Lord's

[5]Neville Clark, *An Approach to the Theology of the Sacraments* (London: SCM Press, 1956), p. 52.

> supper within the Corinthian church had pointed up the abysmal insensitivity of some members to the needs of other members. The Lord's supper had to be seen by them as an act which solidifies the group as a community, called by God which meets in expectation of its Lord and to honor its Lord.[6]

A. Robertson and A. Plummer give A. P. Stanley credit for affirming the church interpretation of 1 Cor. 11:29. It was "the community and fellowship one with another which the Corinthian Christians were so slow to discern."[7]

Significant scholars taking the other side of this issue include A. Robertson and A. Plummer:

> It is not likely that, because the bread symbolizes the many grains of Christians souls united in one Church, *to sōma* here means the body of Christians; still less that it means "the substance" which is veiled in the bread, as some Lutherans interpret.[8]

J. J. Lias said,

> The believer has discerned the fact that it is no ordinary meal in which he is invited to participate, but that in the rite there is a feeding on the Body of Christ.[9]

H. L. Goudge defined "body,"

[6]Carl Holladay, *The First Letter of Paul to the Corinthians*, The Living Word Bible Commentary (Austin, Tex.: Sweet Publishing Co., 1979), p. 151.

[7]Archibald Robertson and Alfred Plummer, *A Critical and Exegetical Commentary on the First Epistle of Paul to the Corinthians*, International Critical Commentary (Edinburgh, Scotland: T. & T. Clark, 1911), p. 252, n*.

[8]Ibid., p. 252.

[9]J. J. Lias, *The First Epistle to the Corinthians*, Cambridge Greek Testament for Schools and Colleges (Cambridge: Cambridge University Press, 1910), p. 133.

> . . . i.e., the glorified humanity of the Lord. . . . The eye of faith must be directed to the Body of the Lord, so as to discriminate it from ordinary food.[10]

F. W. Grosheide commented,

> By not coming to the table in the right manner one does not regard the body (i.e., the body and blood) as it should be regarded.[11]

In summarizing the problem of exegesis of this verse, it would seem to me that the issue turns on the question of context. Is "body" (*sōma*) to be defined by its use in chapter 12 or by its use in the closer context of the passage itself? One has to grant that the present chapter division of the Corinthian letter is not original, yet it would seem to me that the chapter division here is not misplaced. Paul is taking up a new topic in chapter 12, not continuing the one he has previously been discussing. I see no evidence to establish that Paul used *sōma* (body) in two different senses in 1 Cor. 11:24-29, making "the body" to be discerned to be the church.

[10]H. L. Goudge, *The First Epistle to the Corinthians*, Westminster Commentaries, 3d ed. rev. (London: Methuen & Co., 1911), p. 102.

[11]F. W. Grosheide, *Commentary on the First Epistle to the Corinthians*, The New International Commentary on the New Testament (Grand Rapids, Mich.: Wm. B. Eerdmans Publishing Co., 1955), p. 275.

17

"A Cloud of Witnesses"

Hebrews 12:1

The writer of the Epistle to the Hebrews closely connects chapter 12 with chapter 11 by using a Greek coordinating participle, *toigaroun* (wherefore), which occurs elsewhere in the New Testament at the beginning of a sentence only in 1 Thess. 4:8. Its use is a stylistic peculiarity of biblical Greek through Semitic influence. The writer of the Epistle points out that we also are to be as those of the old covenant.

Heb. 12:1 has a number of words, some of which do not occur elsewhere in the New Testament, which merit consideration. "Compassed about" is archaic English for "surrounded." *Nephos* (cloud) occurs only here in the

New Testament though it was earlier used in the Septuagint to render the Hebrew terms *'abh* and *'anan*, both of which designate cloud masses. The more common New Testament term for cloud is *nephelē* which occurs in about sixteen passages. Though the distinction between the two Greek words may not be great, *nephos*, besides its use for clouds of the sky, is used in secular writers for a compact, numberless throng. Homer in the *Iliad* (4.274; 16.66; 17.755; 23.133) has clouds of various things, and Herodotus (8.109) uses *nephos* in the expression translated "a host of men." In Is. 60:8, those returning from exile are said to fly like a cloud. Herodotus' phrase is a close parallel to Heb. 12:1. The term used should be understood as a "host," "multitude," or "crowd" of witnesses. They are those previously mentioned in chapter 11.

THE WITNESSES

Martus was translated into Latin as *testis* and then into English as "witnesses." Its implication is crucial to the meaning of Heb. 12:1. At times *martus* designates witnesses in the legal sense (Mt. 18:16; Acts 7:58; 2 Cor. 13:1; 1 Tim. 5:18; Heb. 10:28). One may contrast these witnesses with false witnesses (*pseudomartures*, Mt. 26:60; 1 Cor. 15:15; *marturas pseudeis*, Acts 6:13). *Martus* also occurs as a figurative term, whether describing God (Rom. 1:9; 2 Cor. 1:23; Phil. 1:8; 1 Thess. 2:5; cf. Wisd. 1:6) or men (1 Thess. 2:10; 1 Tim. 6:12; 2 Tim. 2:3), for anyone who can testify to anything. It includes those who attest events of which they know but have not personally experienced (Lk. 11:48). *Martus* also in the persecuted church becomes one who witnesses to death

(Acts 22:20; Rev. 2:13; 17:6; and probably Rev. 1:5; 3:14).

The significant question concerning Heb. 12:1 is, to what extent does the term have the connotation of "spectator" so that those who have gone before are being declared spectators of our struggles? The Greek word *theoros*, meaning one who is spectator at the games, does not occur in the New Testament; however, *theatron* (spectacle) does occur but has the connotation of being the object of unfriendly looking. The Christian is a spectacle to the world (1 Cor. 4:9). A verb of the same root describes those publicly exposed (Heb. 10:33).

Westcott said that there is no evidence that *martus* was ever used simply in the sense of "spectator," but that it was impossible in Heb. 12:1 to exclude the thought of spectators in the amphitheater. Kittel's *Theological Dictionary* also would not exclude the idea of on-looker; but, is not the challenge of the passage that we are surrounded by those who have suffered, bearing personal testimony to faith, and that their example should give us courage to suffer? Verbs of the same root have been used in Heb. 11:2, 4-5, and 39 for the testimony borne to them. From the context, we look to them rather than their looking on us. Moffatt said, "It is what we see in them, not what they see in us, that is the writer's main point." They are witnesses of the faith he demands of his readers.

Is it not likely that we have made center that which is only possible? Would not the passage lose some of its power if *theatron* (spectator) were substituted for *martus*? Kenneth Taylor's "Since we have such a huge crowd of men of faith watching us from the grandstands," makes central that which is not at all certain.

WEIGHT AND SIN

Like Paul (cf. 1 Cor. 9:24; Gal. 2:2; Phil. 2:16; 3:12ff.; 2 Tim. 2:5; 4:7; cf. Acts 20:24), the writer of the Epistle to the Hebrews uses the figure of the games to describe the Christian's struggles. As the athlete lays aside his clothing, so the Christian must strip off hindrances. The Greek word *ogkos* occurs only in this passage in the New Testament, but occurs in secular Greek from the time of Homer (e.g., in Josephus *War* 4.319; 7.443) for weight, burden, or impediment. The expression "every weight" is general and the writer of the Epistle does not at this point attempt to give specifics for the adjective "every" (*pas*).

The conjunction *kai* (and) is here coordinate rather than explanatory. "Sin" does not explain "weight." "The sin which doth so easily beset us" (*tēn euperistaton hamartian*; RSV: "sin which clings so closely") deserves notice. The textual commentary classes the alternate reading *euperispaston* (easily distracting) as either "a palaeographical error or a deliberate modification"; nevertheless, the NEB carries it as a marginal reading. The inclusion or omission of the definite article in English determines whether the reader thinks of the sin spoken of as specific or generic, and the relevance of the matter in current exegesis is seen when one considers all the sermons he has preached or heard on "*the* besetting sin." Moffatt says, "The article does not imply any specific sin like that of apostasy . . . it is *hamartia* in general." One may compare Heb. 9:26 where Jesus appeared to "put away sin." The word *euperistaton*, which occurs only here in the New Testament, has been the subject of much debate, but most likely means "easily ensnaring."

RUN THE RACE SET BEFORE US

Trechein (to run) occurs in the New Testament in a dozen passages for the literal running of various persons (Mt. 27:48; 28:8; Mk. 5:6; 15:26; Lk. 15:20; 24:12; Jn. 20:2, 4; Rom. 9:16; 1 Cor. 9:24), for the running of horses to battle (Rev. 9:9), and for Paul's metaphorical description of the Christian life as a race (1 Cor. 9:24; Gal. 2:2; cf. Phil. 2:16). The Galatians had been running well (Gal. 5:7). It is the occurrence of *trechein* in Heb. 12:1 that eventually brought English translators around to "race" as the rendering of *agon* which we consider in the next paragraph. The terms "run" and "race" go together. The Greek hautatory subjunctive plural form *trechōmen* which is used justifies the rendering "let us run." The figure of a race for spiritual struggles also occurs in 4 Macc. 14:5: "as if running the course to deathlessness . . . ."

In the final phrase in the verse, the verb *prokeisthai*, which occurs in five New Testament passages, is used. It is rendered in the KJV both as "to be" (2 Cor. 8:12; Jude 2) and as "set before" (Heb. 6:18; 12:1-2). The NEB has "the race for which we are entered." The noun *agōn* occurs in six passages and is rendered "conflict" (Phil. 1:30; Col. 2:1); "contention" (1 Thess. 2:2); "fight" (1 Tim. 6:12; 2 Tim. 4:7); and "race" (Heb. 12:1). In Heb. 12:1, *agōn* was rendered into Latin as *propositum*. This phrase came into English with Wycliffe as "the batel purposid to us." Tyndale, the Great Bible, and the Bishops' Bible all continued with "battle" with various spellings; but the Geneva Bible contributed "the race which is set before us," and that rendering was adopted by the KJV and later translations. It fits the verb "run." The 1611 KJV read, "run unto the race," using a preposition as its

English predecessors (except the Geneva) had. Somewhere along the line of revision since 1611, the KJV was made to harmonize with the Geneva Bible in this detail. The preposition was dropped.

WITH PATIENCE

The Greek phrase *di' hupomonēs* (with patience) also occurs in Rom. 8:25. It passed into Latin as *per patientiam.* Wycliffe followed the Latin with "bi pacience." Tyndale made it to be "with pacience," and with varied spellings (except for the rendering "by patience" of the Rheims) that rendering was used by English translations through the ASV. The RSV and the NIV have "with perseverance"; the NAB, "persevere"; the NEB, "with resolution"; the TEV, "with determination"; and the NKJV, "with endurance." The word "patience" has in current English taken on the meaning of "uncomplaining endurance" which is not the meaning of some New Testament passages (e.g., Jas. 5:7ff.). *Hupomonē* in Greek is that spiritual stickability which enabled the martyrs to die for their faith. The idea of continuous keeping on is most suitable in Heb. 12:1. Already at Heb. 10:36, the reader has been told that he needs "endurance."

The call for perseverance in faith is the intent of the verse. Jesus is the great exemplar of that faith.

18

Those Who Rule

Hebrews 13:7, 17, 24

Our lectureships quite often announce as the topic for discussion "Do Elders Rule?" The speaker, then, with appropriate eloquence and show of eruditeness, will argue on the KJV wording of Heb. 13:7, 17, 24, will smugly conclude that indeed the Scriptures do teach that elders rule, and will insist that all of any contrary opinion are deniers of the Word of God. It never seems to enter the mind to ask: first, if the *hēgoumenoi* of Hebrews are indeed the elders, and second, to ask if "rule" in the sense the speaker is using the term is the sense the Greek *hēgoumenoi* carried in these passages. All the speaker has done is to remind us of the KJV wording of the passages; he has not bothered to ask the more basic question concerning what the passages mean.

I do not think you would find one in ten thousand who knows that Heb. 13:7 and 17 each in 1611 carried the marginal option that is no longer printed: "Or, are the guides." Now the meaning to the modern man of "have the rule over you" and "are guides" is vastly different!

The New Testament is not explicit, but is it possible that the leaders (*hēgoumenoi*) spoken of in these verses are the "elders"? What other possibilities are there? Well, perhaps none if the KJV wording is taken as infallible. But if one starts with the Greek word *hēgemōn*, he might argue that the term includes those from whom one learned the gospel—the teachers. Though I do not wish to argue for preacher's authority, it might even include the preacher in as far as he is a teacher. However, if one is not capable of going back to the KJV wording, I would like to go soft on any suggestion of the preacher's having authority. I would like to supply to them the KJV phrase "usurp authority" (1 Tim. 2:12). They run the churches.

Rather than dealing with current leadership of the church, Heb. 13:7 likely deals with leaders who have already gone to their reward:

> Remember your leaders, those who spoke to you the word of God; consider the outcome of their life, and imitate their faith.

It is the phrase "consider the outcome of their life" that lies back of my suggestion that the verse is speaking of leaders of the past. In this case, *tōn hēgoumenōn humōn* is a participial construction whose time is likely controlled by the aorist verb *elalēsan* (who spoke) which follows it in the sentence. It speaks of those from whom the readers learned the gospel.

However, in verse 17 the *hēgoumenoi* are to be obeyed and submitted to. Then, in verse 24 one is called on to "Greet all your leaders and all the saints." In this verse, a distinction is made between the "leaders" (*hēgoumenoi*) and the saints (*hagioi*).

From the general association of *hēgesthai* with ruling, one is tempted to conclude that here at last we have indisputable authority for a ruling concept in connection with the leadership of the church. However, before one makes up his mind in which of the varieties of meaning he will understand the use of *hēgesthai* in Heb. 13:7, 17, 24, there are some questions he needs to ask. Did Paul have ruling authority over Barnabas when he was the "chief speaker" (*ho hēgoumenos tou logou*) of the pair (Acts 14:12)? Furthermore, what is the position of Judas Barsabbas and Silas in the church of Jerusalem when they are "leading men among the brethren" (*andras hēgoumenous en tois adelphois*; Acts 15:22)? Does the designation mean that they ruled over the brothers, or does it mean that they were outstanding men in this fellowship? What is to be made of, "But you are not to be like that. Instead the greatest among you should be like the youngest, and the one who rules [*ho hēgoumenos*; KJV: chief; RSV: leader] as the one who serves" (*ho diakonōn*; Lk. 22:26, NIV).

19

The Priesthood

1 Peter 2:5-9

> And like living stones be yourselves built into a spiritual house, to be a holy priesthood, to offer spiritual sacrifices acceptable to God through Jesus Christ. . . . But you are a chosen race, a royal priesthood, a holy nation, God's own people, that you may declare the wonderful deeds of him who called you out of darkness into his marvelous light (1 Pet. 2:5-9).

The idea of the priest as a religious functionary is not unique to the Bible, but goes back in the Middle East to the dawn of history. Priests were known in the Mesopotamian, Egyptian, and Canaanite areas. Priests are first met in the Bible in the persons of Melchizedek, priest of God Most High (*'el 'elyon*) in Salem (Jerusalem?; Gen. 14:18); of Potiphera, priest of On, who became father-in-law to Joseph (Gen. 41:45, 50); of other Egyptian priests (Gen. 47:22); and of Reuel, priest of Midian, who became father-in-law to Moses (Ex. 2:16). Later, Micah, an Ephraimite, consecrated one of his sons to be his own priest (Judg. 17:5) but then afterward chose a Levite (Judg. 17:10). That priest migrated to Laish with the Danites. Jonathan, son of Gershom, son of Moses, and his sons remained priests in the tribe of Dan (Judg. 18:30). David's sons are said to be priests (RSV; KJV: chief rulers; NIV: royal advisors) in one passage (2 Sam. 8:18).

TERMINOLOGY

In biblical Hebrew the term *kohen* designates the priests of the Lord as well as Egyptian (Gen. 41:45; 47:22), Canaanite (2 Kings 10:19; 11:18), Philistine (1 Sam. 5:5; 6:2), Moabite (Jer. 48:7), and Ammonite (Jer. 49:3) priests. Another noun, *komer/kemarim*, occurs three times, always in the plural in the Old Testament (2 Kings 23:5; Hos. 10:5, and Zeph. 1:4), for the priests of false gods. In the Greek Bible, the first of these terms becomes *hiereus*, which term is later used in the New Testament; the second noun is transliterated *chōmerim* in 2 Kings 23:5, but is *hiereus* in Zeph. 1:4. The etymology of the word *kohen* is uncertain. In Canaan, the god Dagon had his priests (1 Sam. 5:5; 6:2), as did Baal (2 Kings 10:19; 23:5).

Priests existed in Israel before Sinai (Ex. 19:22, 24), but then in the provision of the law of Moses the Levitical tribe, Aaron and his sons, were to serve in the priesthood.

Their priesthood is called "perpetual" (Ex. 40:15; Num. 25:13; cf. Jer. 33:18, 21); however, Nadab and Abihu committed a ritual offense and perished (Lev. 10:1-7; Num. 3:4; 26:61), making appointment of other sons necessary.

The remainder of the Levitical clan were also considered a sort of priesthood (Josh. 18:7), but they were primarily priestly assistants (cf. Numbers 4). Korah's rebellion in the desert is interpreted as a transgression of the priesthood (Num. 16:10). Of the Aaronites, Aaron himself (cf. Ps. 99:6), then his son Eleazar, and afterward the legal head of the family were high priests. The high priest was chosen by descent and enjoyed a life appointment.

Though participation in the priesthood came by inheritance, the individual priest was inducted into his position of service by a consecration which, if literally translated, would be a "filling of the hands" (Ex. 28:41; 29:9; 32:29; Lev. 8:33; Num. 3:3; Judg. 17:5, 12; 1 Kings 13:33). There was an elaborate ceremony (Ex. 28:41ff.; 29:7f.; 30:30f.; Lev. 8:12f., 33). The priest is said to be anointed (Ex. 40:12-15). He could have no physical defect (Lev. 21:16-24), could not shave his head or beard (Lev. 21:5), and could not touch the corpse even of a close relative (Lev. 21:1). He could not marry a harlot or one who had been divorced from her husband (Lev. 21:7). He must abstain from wine and alcohol when in service (Lev. 10:8-11). He wore special clothing when in service (Ex. 28), was set apart (Num. 8:14; Deut. 10:8), and was considered sanctified for his task (Lev. 21:6). Saul's servants shrank from his command to kill the priests of Nob (1 Sam. 22:17).

Priests served at special shrines. The Levite who accompanied the Danites came to Laish, also called Dan

(Judg. 18:20). Eli was at Shiloh (1 Sam. 1-4) until his house was rejected by the Lord (1 Sam. 12:27-36); but his grandson, Ahijah, accompanied Saul (1 Sam. 14:3, 18). Eleazar was at Kiriath-jearim (1 Sam. 7:1ff.), Ahimelech and others at Nob (1 Sam. 21:2; 22:9), and Abiathar from Anathoth fled to David (1 Sam. 22:23) and later served at Jerusalem (1 Kings 2:27). David also had Ira, son of Jair, as priest (2 Sam. 20:26). Zadok served at Jerusalem (1 Kings 1:38; 4:4). The prophet Jeremiah was descended from priests at Anathoth (Jer. 1:1ff.). After the division of the kingdom, Jeroboam appointed priests for the high places like Bethel and Dan (1 Kings 12:31; 2 Chron. 11:15). At Bethel, Amos encountered Amaziah (Amos 7:10ff.). Jehu's revolt included slaying the priests of Ahab (2 Kings 10:11) as well as those of the high places (2 Kings 10:19). Josiah, in his reform, slaughtered the priests of the high places of Samaria (2 Kings 23:20) and burned the bones of the priests of the high places (2 Chron. 34:5).

By the time of Ezra's and Nehemiah's return from the Exile, the priests numbered several thousand (Ezra 2:36ff.; Neh. 7:39ff.). Those who defiled themselves by intermarriage were put out of the priesthood (Ezra 2:62; Neh. 7:64; 13:29). Nehemiah counted this reform among his greatest acts (Neh. 13:29f.). David is given credit for having divided the priests into twenty-four classes (1 Chron. 24:7-19) who lived in the villages (cf. Neh. 11:3, 12), but who functioned in turn in Jerusalem for a period of one week before returning home. Under this arrangement, Zechariah of the New Testament period is said to belong to the course of Abijah (1 Chron. 24:10; Lk. 1:5, 8).[1]

[1]Josephus *Antiquities* 7.14.7 (365).

THE PRIESTHOOD IN ACTION

Whereas in earlier times the head of the family sacrificed (Gen. 12:9; 15:9; 35:6; 46:1), under the law the priests conducted the sacrifices (Deut. 33:10; Jer. 33:18). Details are given for five sorts of sacrifices in Leviticus 1-7 (cf. Heb. 5:1; 8:3). Animals, vegetables, oil, wheat, salt, and incense were offered. Two priests sounded the trumpet at the time of sacrifice (Num. 10:1, 8; 2 Chron. 29:26-28). The Levites also participated in the worship in various ways, but not in the actual rites and sacrifices. They had charge of the vessels and prepared things for the priests (Num. 4:1ff.; 1 Chron. 23:28-32). It was granted by the Pharisees in the New Testament period that the tasks of sacrifice when discharged on the Sabbath did not make the priests guilty of breaking the Sabbath (Mt. 12:5; cf. Mk. 2:26; Lk. 6:4).

The priests were responsible for keeping the lay people from entering the tabernacle (Num. 3:38) and later maintained the sanctity of the temple. The priests were subordinate to the king, but watched the gates of the temple (2 Kings 11:10) and received gifts for its repair (2 Kings 22:4). Jehoiada was responsible for the overthrow of Athaliah (2 Kings 11:4ff.; 2 Chron. 23:1). Hilkiah managed the fund of the temple (2 Kings 22:3ff.). Pashur maintained order there (Jer. 20:1), and King Uzziah's presumption in offering sacrifice was opposed by the high priest and eighty other priests (2 Chron. 26:16-20).

As wearers of the ephod (likely an article of clothing rather than being a box which some interpreters have supposed it to be), the priests gave answers by means of the Urim and Thummim (the sacred lots; Num. 27:21; 1 Sam. 14:41-42) to those who inquired of the will of God (cf. 1 Sam. 23:9; 30:7-8). Eleazar gave Joshua oracles (Num. 27:20f.) and served with him as leader (Num. 34:17). Micah's Levite gave the Danites an answer to their question (Judg. 17:5; 18:5ff.); David obtained oracles at Nob (1 Sam. 22:15); Ahijah gave Saul an answer (1 Sam. 14:18, 41ff.); and Abiathar guided David (1 Sam. 23:9ff.; 30:7ff.). After the Exile, there was no priest to consult the Urim and Thummim (Ezra 2:63; Neh. 7:65).

The priests declared persons and objects clean and unclean after examination (Lev. 13:2ff.; Deut. 24:8; cf. Lk. 17:14). The priests were also entrusted with the law (*torah*; Deut. 17:11; 33:10) and were the teachers of the people (Lev. 10:11; Ezek. 44:23; Hag. 2:11). They were the messengers of the Lord (Mal. 2:7), but they are indicted by the prophets for their failure to discharge this function properly (Jer. 18:18; 23:11; Ezek. 7:26; 22:26; Hos. 4:4, 6, 9; Mic. 3:11; Zeph. 3:4; Mal. 2:1-9). If one contrasted the priest and the prophet, he would say that the priest handed on traditional knowledge. The priests at the sanctuary decided otherwise unsolvable cases (Deut. 17:8-13).

The high priest (Num. 35:25, 28), initiated into his term of service by anointing with oil (Ex. 29:29; Lev. 4:5; 8:10f., 30; 10:7) and an elaborate ceremony, had a headband engraved with the words "Holy to the Lord" (Ex. 28:36) and he wore special robes (Ex. 28:17-29:21). He was set apart for the holy things (1 Chron. 23:13), making him separate from profane things. He is called "chief among his brethren" (Lev. 21:10). The high priest officiated on the Day of Atonement (Leviticus 16), making atonement first for his own sins and then for the sins of the people. Only he went into the most holy place (Mishnah *Yoma*), and he entered only on the Day of Atonement. He was an intermediary between man and

God (Heb. 5:1). Liability for bloodshed terminated with his death (Num. 35:25, 28, 32). In addition to being called "high priest" (*kohen haggadhol*), he is in a few places called "head priest" (*kohen haro'sh*; 2 Kings 25:18; 2 Chron. 19:11). After the mention of the chief priest in the Pentateuch, this rank of priest is only infrequently mentioned in the Old Testament (2 Kings 12:10[11]; 22:4, 8; 23:4) in the pre-exilic narratives.

Allotted cities (Num. 35:1-8; Josh. 21:1ff.; 1 Chron. 6:54ff.), but not having a share in the land distribution (Num. 18:20), the priests were supported by the tithes, firstfruits (Deut. 18:1-5), firstborn animals, and portions of various sacrifices (Num. 18:8ff.; 1 Sam. 2:13ff.; 2 Kings 12:16; 2 Chron. 31:4ff.; Neh. 10:38ff.; 12:44f.). Theirs also was the right to eat the showbread from the sanctuary (Mk. 2:26).

THE PRIESTHOOD FROM THE EXILE TO THE NEW TESTAMENT

The priestly upper classes were exiled by the Assyrians and Babylonians (2 Kings 17:27ff.; 25:18). After the Exile, Joshua is the representative of the surviving priesthood as Zerubbabel is the governor descended from David. The two stand side by side (Zech. 4:3ff.; 6:9-15; cf. Ezra 3:1-6; Haggai 1-2), and the priest seems the equal of the governor (Hag. 1:1, 12, 14; 2:2, 4); they are the two anointed (Zech. 4:14).

The priestly group, no longer Aaronites, assumed secular power during the Maccabean period when the priests became kings (cf. 1 Macc. 10:20f.). Simon is praised as among the greatest of them (Sir. 50:1ff.). In this way, by New Testament times priests had civil as well as religious authority. High priests were then made and unmade by secular rulers at their whim so that twenty-eight served between 37 B. C. and A. D. 67. They seem to have been chosen from a few prominent families. Annas (Lk. 3:2; Jn. 18:13, 24; Acts 4:6), five of his sons, a grandson, and his son-in-law (Caiaphas; cf. Lk. 3:2), and Ananias (Acts 23:2; 24:1)[2] occupied the position over much of the New Testament period. Jesus never challenged the sacrificial system or the position of the priesthood; however, the triumphal entry into Jerusalem and the cleansing of the temple did bring him into a clash with certain portions of their temple arrangements.

THE NEW TESTAMENT ASPECT

In the Epistle to the Hebrews, the writer expounds the theme that Jesus, by his divine appointment (Heb. 5:4), is a priest after the order of Melchizedek (cf. Psalm 110). He is the great high priest (Heb. 4:14; 10:21) functioning in the sanctuary not pitched by men's hands, which is heaven itself. To his priesthood, there is no end. He has no need to offer sacrifice daily; one time for all (Heb. 9:12, 26; 10:10, 14) in his death on the cross he has made an atonement in the offering of his own blood as a sweet smelling offering to God (Eph. 5:1-2). The benefits extend to all mankind. He continuously intercedes in our behalf. This high priest, through himself, has given access to the throne on high to all his people (Heb. 10:19-22). They can draw near and receive grace (Heb. 4:16). The altar (Heb. 13:10) which the Christian has is likely that where Christ has made his atoning sacrifice.

[2]Ibid., 20.5.1 (103).

THE LIVING STONE

The Lord was worshiped first at the tabernacle (which was in essence a portable tent) but later was worshiped in the temple which was a permanent structure made of prepared stones so that no sound of hammer or iron tool was heard on the building site. It was made of non-living materials—of stone and wood—as also were pagan temples. In contrast, in a passage (1 Pet. 2:4-9) replete with words from the Greek Old Testament, God's spiritual (*pneumatikos*) house (another term for the Lord's church: 1 Cor. 3:16-17; Eph. 2:20-22; Heb. 3:6) is not made of ordinary stones, but is of living stones; that is, it is of persons redeemed with blood (cf. 1 Pet. 1:18-19). A spiritual house is one indwelt by the Spirit.[3]

The English versions differ over whether the Greek word for "come" should be interpreted as a participle of progressive action (KJV; ASV; NIV) or as a participle with imperative force (RSV). The source of the phrase (1 Pet. 2:4) is perhaps from Ps. 34(33):5(6), which psalm verse has just been cited by 1 Peter (2:3; cf. 3:10-12). The Greek verb is frequently used in the Septuagint for drawing near to God in worship to offer prayer and sacrifice. It may be used either for the people's drawing near or the priest's drawing near.[4]

The expression "living stone" is not used elsewhere but may be compared with "living bread" (Jn. 6:51), "living hope" (1 Pet. 1:3), and "living word" (1 Pet. 1:23). Of these living stones, Jesus, who dies no more (Rom. 6:9) and is a life-giving spirit (1 Cor. 15:45), is first mentioned. "Stone" has an Old Testament background where it is an

[3]Gustav Stählin, "*Orgē*," *TDNT*, 5:435.
[4]Johannes Schneider, "*Proserchomai*," *TDNT*, 2:684.

epithet both of Abraham, as the ancestor of Israel (Is. 51:1), and of the Lord himself (Deut. 32:4, 18, 30-31; 1 Sam. 2:2; 2 Sam. 22:2, 47; Ps. 18:2, 31, 46; 28:1; 42:9; 62:2, 6; 78:35; 89:26; 94:22; 95:1; Is. 17:10). Elsewhere Christ is called the "spiritual rock" (1 Cor. 10:4).[5]

But mindful of the fact that the church is said to be built upon the foundation of the apostles and prophets with Jesus Christ as the cornerstone (Eph. 2:20), it is not surprising that the writer of 1 Peter finds apt descriptions in Ps. 118:22 and Is. 28:16 which speak of a stone laid in Zion. Already in the Gospels Jesus had contrasted the plan of God with that of the Jewish people under the figure of the rejected cornerstone (Mt. 21:42; Mk. 12:10; Lk. 20:17). Peter also used the figure in Acts 4:11. The image envisions prepared stones which are then fitted into place on the construction site. In this figurative way, Jesus' death and rejection (cf. Mk. 8:31; Lk. 9:22; cf. Is. 53:3) at the hands of the Jewish leaders is contrasted with his exaltation at God's hands. This contrast is emphasized in early Christian preaching (Acts 2:23-24, 32-33; 4:11-12; 5:30-31). As Peter is said to be an offense (Mt. 16:23), so the word about Christ was a cause of offense (1 Cor. 1:23).[6]

TWO EPITHETS FOR THE PRIESTHOOD

Two epithets are used to describe the stone. It is elect and precious in the sight of God. The first of these terms is used in the phrase "elect angels" (1 Tim. 5:21) and is also used for Christians in the address of 1 Peter (1:1).

[5]See B. Lindars, *New Testament Apologetic* (Philadelphia, Pa.: Westminster Press, 1961), pp. 169ff.

[6]Joachim Jeremias, "*Akrogōniaios*," *TDNT*, 1:792-94.

The second word, "precious," is taken from the Old Testament quotation (Is. 28:16) used in 1 Pet. 2:6.

The impact of the Lord's coming on two groups is contrasted. To the believer, he is precious; but to the unbeliever, he is a rock of stumbling (cf. Is. 8:14-15; Jer. 6:21; Hos. 14:9). Paul uses this figure for the Jewish experience in confronting the Gospel (Rom. 9:32-33). As the sun hardens cement but melts butter, so the stone has two different impacts. Some believe on him and are not put to shame; but the masses were offended both at his teaching and his failure to fit their preconceived picture of what sort of program he should carry out. That which had been the rock on which they built became the stone on which they stumbled (1 Cor. 1:23; Gal. 5:11). They disobeyed the word (cf. 1 Pet. 1:23, 25).

As the various English versions reflect, the meaning of *akrogōniaios* (Eph. 2:20; 1 Pet. 2:6; cf. Is. 28:16) is disputed. Some see it as the cornerstone holding the wall together; others as the keystone which completes the arch and holds it in place or the stone over the door. In any case, it is a most significant stone.[7]

Not only is the Lord "that living stone" on which the building rests, but Christians also are "living stones" which make up the superstructure of this building. The term "living stones" has no equivalent in the New Testament, but the closest parallel in idea is in Eph. 2:20 where Christians, though not called "stones," are a part of the building.[8] The idea of people as stones was also known in Qumran.[9] Christianity has no holy places and no holy buildings made of stones and mortar. The people themselves comprise the temple of the Lord where he is

[7]Cf. *Ep. Barnabas* 6.2.
[8]Cf. Ignatius *To the Ephesians* 9.1
[9]4QpIsa[d], frag i; cf. 1QH 6:25ff.

worshiped. His house is his church (1 Tim. 3:15).[10]

A ROYAL PRIESTHOOD

Not only do Christians make up the temple of God, but they are also its priesthood. It is against the Old Testament background of the priesthood which we have surveyed that the statements of the Epistle of Peter take on meaning. The church, which is the Lord's body, is a spiritual house (2 Cor. 6:16; Eph. 2:19-22; 1 Pet. 2:5;). It is the shrine or the temple of the living God (1 Cor. 3:16) where his people who have been made "a kingdom, priests unto God" (Rev. 1:6; 5:10) carry out their service to him.

With Christ as the one mediator between God and man, and with the new and living way being opened (Heb. 10:20) giving direct access through Christ (Heb. 13:15; cf. 1 Pet. 2:5) to the throne of God, the child of God has no need that someone discharge for him an additional sacerdotal ministry; nor is there provision for such in the New Testament. The term "priest" is used for the priests under the law and for pagan priests, but does not describe a special class in the Christian group. The Christian himself is a royal priest, and the combination of Christians make up the holy priesthood. In a sense, the dream of Is. 61:6 (cf. Ex. 19:6) where all Israelites become priests is accomplished; however, the Christian is not said to serve as a priest in behalf of someone else.

The writer of 1 Peter assigns to the Christian the functions the priest discharged under the Mosaic system, to be described either as a "holy priesthood" (1 Pet. 2:5;

[10]Cf. Otto Michel, "*Oikos*," *TDNT*, 5:125-28.

2 Macc. 2:17-18)[11] or as a "royal priesthood" (1 Pet. 2:9). With the atoning sacrifice already accomplished in the death of Jesus, the service of this priesthood is that of offering gifts and sacrifices (Heb. 5:1), not that of making an atonement. Its sacrifices are "spiritual sacrifices" (1 Pet. 2:5; cf. 1 Cor. 10:3-4: spiritual rock) to be offered "through Jesus Christ" (cf. Acts 4:12; Rom. 1:8; 16:27; Col. 3:17; 1 Tim. 2:5; Heb. 7:25). The virtual synonym to *pneumatikos* is *logikos* (Rom. 12:1; 1 Pet. 2:2). The idea of spiritual sacrifices is already found in the Old Testament (Ps. 4:5; 50:13-14, 23; 51:17; 141:2; Is. 1:11-15; Hos. 6:6; Mic. 6:6-8) and is also developed in Qumran literature.[12]

The nature of the sacrifices of this holy priesthood is not spelled out in 1 Peter. Elsewhere in Scripture, the Christian is called upon to offer his body a "living sacrifice" as a "spiritual [KJV: reasonable] service."[13] A purposeful contrast must be implied between the offering of an animal which was killed according to the law and the life lived in God's service. The first requires less of the worshiper than does the second. With the Christian raised from the dead (Rom. 6:4), he is called upon to make a total commitment of life in holy living to God, maintaining "holy conduct" (cf. 1 Pet. 1:15f.). His life must be a sweet savor to God (2 Cor. 2:15). Paul's life was a sacrificial offering freely given (Phil. 2:17; cf. 2 Tim. 4:6), and the Philippians made an offering of themselves (Phil. 2:17).

The gifts presented by the Philippians to Paul, when they aided him in his preaching, are described in sacrificial imagery—"a fragrant offering, a sacrifice

[11]Cf. Gerhard Kittel, "*Doxa*," *TDNT*, 2:249f.
[12]1QS 8:4, 5; 9:3ff.; 10:8, 14; 4QFlor 1:6f.
[13]Hermann Strathmann, "*Latreuō*," *TDNT*, 4:61ff.

acceptable and pleasing to God" (Phil. 4:18). This same term, "fragrant offering," is elsewhere used for Jesus' offering of himself (Eph. 5:2). Doing good and sharing are said to be sacrifices pleasing to God (Heb. 13:16). A sacrificial term (*leitourgein*) is used for the collection sent to the poor in Jerusalem (Rom. 15:27; 2 Cor. 9:12).

The songs and prayers of the Christian are also described in that imagery: "Through him then let us continually offer up a sacrifice of praise to God, that is, the fruit of lips that acknowledge his name" (Heb. 13:15). Preparation for this concept is seen in the petition of the psalmist that his prayers be as bowls of incense or as the evening sacrifice before the Lord (Ps. 141:2; cf. Lk. 1:10). It is further developed in the idea that the bowls of incense seen in the Apocalypse are the prayers of the saints (Rev. 8:3). The Qumran community said, "The prayer of the upright is like a pleasing sacrifice."[14] It also said, "A right offering of lips is a righteous savor and a perfect way of life is a free-will offering to God."[15] However, Qumran sacrifices had an atoning function. Qumran did not know the offering made by Christ or offerings through him. The above cited activities make clear that there are ample "spiritual sacrifices" to be offered by the Christian. The idea that the communion has a sacrificial nature is not suggested in the New Testament, but is a post-biblical theological development. There is no suggestion that the above acts atone for sin.

[14]CD 11:20f.
[15]1QS 9:3ff.; cf. 8:4; 4QFlor 1:6f.

DESCRIPTIVE EPITHETS

The descriptive epithets for the Christian (now the New Israel; cf. Gal. 6:16) used in 1 Peter are borrowed from descriptions of Israel in the Old Testament. The "chosen race" (1 Pet. 1:2; 2:6) takes us back to Old Testament concepts of the election of Israel (cf. Ex. 19:6; Deut. 7:6-7; Is. 43:10, 20; 44:1-2). The idea of Christians being a race (*genos*) may be connected with the idea of their being born anew (1 Pet. 1:23); but it set the stage for the later descriptions of them as a third race.[16]

Turning on the unsolved question of whether *basileion* is a noun or an adjective, the "royal priesthood" may suggest either people who are both kings and priests at the same time (cf. Rev. 1:6; 5:10) or priests who belong to and are in the service of a king. The Greek word for "royal" occurs elsewhere in the New Testament only at Lk. 7:25 where it modifies "house." The first of these interpretations suggested above is more in keeping with Rev. 1:6; 5:10; and it makes this verse set forth four attributes. Whichever interpretation is chosen, the concept goes back to the Old Testament term "a kingdom of priests" (Ex. 19:6; cf. Jub. 16:18; 33:20; T. Levi 11:4-6, Gk. frag.). Christians are a body of priests who have been purchased (Acts 20:28; 1 Cor. 6:20; 7:23). They are separated from other nations and are consecrated to the service of God. They have an obligation to live lives of holiness; but that obligation does not eliminate the need for them to be admonished (1 Pet. 1:15).

The epithet "holy nation" comes from Ex. 19:6 and echoes Deut. 7:6; 14:2, 21. The demands made in Leviticus were designed to make a holy nation of Israel for the holy

[16]Aristides *Apology* 2.15; Tertullian *Ad nationes* 1.8.20.

God—"You shall therefore be holy, for I [the Lord your God] am holy" (Lev. 11:44-45; 1 Pet. 1:16). The phrase "a people for God's own possession" (KJV: a peculiar people) comes from Is. 43:21 and echoes the promise to Israel: "I will take you for my people, and I will be your God" (Ex. 6:6-7; 19:5; Deut. 7:6; 14:2; 26:18; Is. 43:21; Hag. 2:9; Mal. 3:17; Acts 20:28; Eph. 1:14; Tit. 2:14). This new people are those purchased by the blood of his son (1 Pet. 2:19; cf. Tit. 2:14).

If, however, one concludes that his place of privilege is not also a call to responsibility, he has missed the thrust of 1 Pet. 2:5-9. Christians have come out of darkness (the realm of sin: Jn. 8:12; Rom. 2:19; 13:12; Eph. 6:12) into marvelous light (cf. Acts 26:18; Eph. 5:8; Col. 1:13). From being no people (Hos. 1:6, 9-10; 2:23; Rom. 9:25-26), they have become the people of God (cf. Acts 15:14ff.; Rom. 9:25; Heb. 4:9; Rev. 18:4). The change from heathenism is drastic (Acts 26:18; Eph. 5:8; Col. 1:13). The term "people" is at times (Acts 26:17, 23; Rom. 15:10) used as an opposite to "Gentiles."

The purpose of the choice is "that you may declare the wonderful deeds of him who called you out of darkness into his marvelous light." The phrase here used for declaring is from Is. 42:21. The Mosaic priests had a teaching function. It was to be a "light to the nations" that Israel was earlier chosen (Is. 41:6), and the Qumran community had the priests declare the righteous deeds of God.[17] If the royal priesthood fails to teach the unlearned, its guilt is no less than that charged by the prophets against the Aaronic priesthood. The outcome will be that which is threatened by Hosea: "My people are destroyed for lack of knowledge; because you have

[17] 1QS 1:21.

rejected knowledge, I reject you from being a priest to me" (Hos. 4:6).

BIBLIOGRAPHY

Baehr, J. "Priest, High Priest." In *A Theological Dictionary to the New Testament*, 3:32-44. Edited by Colin Brown. Grand Rapids: Zondervan Publishing House, 1978.

Best, Ernest. "1 Peter II.4-10—A Reconsideration." *Novum Testamentum* 11 (October 1969):270-93.

________. "Spiritual Sacrifice: General Priesthood in the New Testament." *Interpretation* 14 (July 1960):271-99.

Elliott, J. H. *The Elect and the Holy* (Supplements to *Novum Testamentum XII*). Leiden, 1966.

McKelvey, R. J. "Christ the Cornerstone." *New Testament Studies* 8 (July 1962):352-59.

Moran, W. L. "A Kingdom of Priests." In *The Bible in Current Catholic Thought*, pp. 7-20. Edited by John L. McKenzie. New York: Herder and Herder, 1962.

Moule, C. F. D. "Sanctuary and Sacrifice in the Church of the New Testament." *Journal of Theological Studies*, n.s., no. 1 (April 1950):29-41.

20

"Putting Away" and Divorce

A recent effort to justify remarriage of divorced people which insists that familiar Old Testament and New Testament passages are not dealing with divorce but with forcible expulsion or cruel abandonment of wives by husbands has come to my attention. The author attempts to make a distinction between "send away" and "divorce" in both Old Testament and New Testament vocabulary. According to him, Jesus was prohibiting multiple marriages where there had been no divorce but gave no prohibition of remarriage of those properly divorced.

The author's first distinction is between *shalach* (send

away) and *kerithuth* (divorcement) which occurs in Deut. 24:1, 4 for the bill of divorce. He insists that *shalach* is the cruel, harsh expelling without a divorce after which other marriages are contracted. One notices that Abraham sent (*shalach*) Hagar away (Gen. 21:14); but it is particularly Mal. 2:16: "For I hate divorce [*shalach*]," that draws the author's attention. He insists that the translation "divorce" is erroneous and that "send away" (that is, without a divorce) is the proper term for what God hates.

In evaluating this case, one first must ask if the writer of Deuteronomy was merely prohibiting the abandonment of the woman whose virginity is slandered by her husband (Deut. 22:19) and of the woman who has been seduced prior to marriage (Deut. 22:29). The verb *shalach* occurs in both of these laws. Would it have been all right to divorce them if the proper papers had been given?

The putting away of women at the time of the return from the Exile is described by a causative form of *yatsa'* (to cause to go out; Ezra 10:3, 19). The divorced woman is called the *gerushah* (the expelled, from *garash*; Lev. 21:14; 22:13; Num. 30:10; Ezek. 44:22), and the abandoned woman is named *'azubhah* (Is. 62:4). Is it merely the abandoned woman or is it the divorced one who is prohibited to the high priest (Lev. 21:14; Ezek. 44:22)?

The author's fallacy is most obvious when one considers *kerithuth* (from *karath*, to cut off) which occurs in three divorce settings for the bill of divorce (Deut. 24:1, 3; Is. 50:1; Jer. 3:8). The Lord asks, "Where is your mother's bill of divorce [*sepher kerithuth*] with which I put her away [*shalach*]?" (Is. 50:1). Again he says, "She saw that for all the adulteries of the faithless one, Israel, I had sent [*shalach*] her away with a decree of divorce [*sepher kerithuth*]" (Jer. 3:8).

These two passages make crystal clear that an effort to make a distinction between *shalach* and *kerithuth* with one meaning abandonment and the other divorce cannot stand. Both terms here refer to the same action.

Since the author's struggles with the New Testament are based upon his fallacy with the Old Testament, they are not more successful. He parallels *shalach* of the Old Testament (which he has already misinterpreted) to *apoluō* in the New Testament; however, the Greek Bible does not use *apoluō* in any of the Old Testament passages, as we will see.

The author observes that the KJV translated *apoluō* as "put away" in all eleven New Testament cases except one—that of Mt. 5:32 which reads "divorce." He charges that all English thinking has been colored by this KJV flaw, causing all (even the dictionary makers) to think of "divorce" as being the subject of all the New Testament passages. The ASV renders Mt. 5:32 as "put away," which the author likes; and he concludes that all of these passages are dealing with abandonment, and not with divorce. He sees subsequent marriage after abandonment prohibited but not after *apostasion* which he defines as "divorce."

One cannot deny that the KJV has colored (and sometimes in error) all our thinking; but whether this case is such an instance merits another look. *Apostasion* occurs in the New Testament in only three passages (Mt. 5:31; 19:7; Mk. 10:4), all of which echo Deut. 24:1, 3. The Bauer *Lexicon* comments, "The consequent giving up of one's claims explains the meaning which the word acquires in Jewish circles."[1]

[1]Bauer, *Greek-English Lexicon*, p. 97.

The Greek Old Testament uses *apostellein* (send away; Gen. 21:14) and *exapostellein* (send away; Deut. 22:19, 29; Mal. 2:16) for the *shalach* passages we have already examined; however, the second word (*exapostellein*) is also the verb used in Deut. 24:1, 3; Is. 50:1; and Jer. 3:8 for the dismissal of the woman who has the *biblion apostasiou* (bill of divorce), leaving no linguistic basis for a distinction between the cases where the bill is specifically mentioned and where it is not. Ezra 10:3 uses *ekballein* (expel) and Ezra 10:19 uses *ekpherein* (bring out) in describing the post-exilic divorces.

The divorced woman is described by a passive participle of the verb *ekballein* (to cast out; Lev. 21:14; 22:13; Num. 30:10; Ezek. 44:22), and the abandoned one is named *Erēmos* (desolate; Is. 62:4).

The writer's New Testament case stands or falls on the validity of his asserted definition of *apoluō* as meaning "put away [*apoluō*] his wife without bothering with a written divorce." He claims,

> *Apoluō* indicated that women were enslaved, put away, with no rights, no recourse; deprived of the basic right of monogamous marriage. *Apostasion* ended marriage and permitted a legal subsequent marriage. The paper makes a difference.

He asserts that the Greek word *apoluō* did not include a writing of divorce for the woman: "She, technically, would still be married."

Here, we have a case of a man's creating a definition which supports a distinction congenial to his case and then proceeding to chase his own tail by assuming that he has established his contention. There is no possible way for him to establish the limited definition of *apoluō* which he is championing. *Apoluō* means "to set free" and is used in other settings than divorce ones. It also means to dismiss a wife and is used in this sense by Dionysius of Halicarnasus 2.25.7 and Diodorus Siculus 12.18.1.[2] The fallacy of the writer we are reviewing is in assuming that *apoluō* in the New Testament cases where the *biblion apostasiou* is mentioned has a different meaning from the eight cases where it is not. Such a distinction will not stand.

Josephus, commenting on Deut. 22:13ff., used the verb *apopempein* for the dismissal;[3] he also uses *apopempein* for the putting away of the slave girl by Pheroras,[4] as well as for his own divorce.[5] In discussing Deut. 24:1, he uses *diazeuchthēnai* (to be disjoined).[6] He describes how Salome sent Costobarus a document dissolving (*apoluō*) their marriage,[7] and she then is described by the passive participle *diachōrizein* (separated). This variety should caution against making hard and fast distinctions that are not explicitly mentioned.

Hermas, in the second Christian century, continues the use of the gospel term *apoluō*[8] in discussing divorce. It is not conceivable that Hermas, who knows the gospel passage, could, in his command about the immoral wife "Let him put [*apoluō*] her away," mean what our author is contending for—the harsh, cruel dismissal without a bill of divorce. Smatterers in Hebrew and Greek should not set themselves up to challenge the reliability of all the Greek and Hebrew lexicons, not to mention all rabbinic discussion of a question.

[2]See I. H. Marshall, "Divorce," in *Dictionary of New Testament Theology*, ed. Colin Brown (Grand Rapids, Mich.: Zondervan, 1975), 1:505-7.

[3]Josephus *Antiquities* 4.8.23 (247).

[4]Ibid., 16.8.3 (198).

[5]Josephus *Life* 426.

[6]Josephus *Antiquities* 4.8.23 (253).

[7]Ibid., 15.7.10 (259).

[8]Hermas *Mandate* 4.1.6, 7.

21

The Intermediate State Of the Dead

DEATH[1]

Death (*maveth*; Gk., *thanatos*), an ever-present feature of life common to all men from the death of Abel onward,

[1]Edmund F. Sutcliffe, *The Old Testament and the Future Life* (London: Burns, Oates & Washbourne, Ltd., 1946), 201 pp.; Robert Martin-Achard, *De la mort a la Resurrection d'apres l'Ancien Testament* (Paris: Delachaux et Niestle, 1955), 187 pp.; George Mark Elliott, "Future Life in the Old Testament," *The Seminary Review*, 3 (Spring-Summer, 1957):41-93; Nicholas J. Tromp, *Primitive Conceptions of Death and the Nether World in the Old Testament* (Rome: Pontifical Biblical Institute, 1969), 241 pp.; Ryder Smith, *The Bible Doctrine of the Hereafter* (London: Epworth Press, 1958), pp. 32-65, 86-95, 157-173.

brought the need in Palestine for the quick disposal of the body. Burial (root, *qabhar*) might take place in an especially purchased cave like that of Machpelah (Genesis 23), or might be beside the way if death occurred while the family was traveling. Each archaeological period of Palestine from prehistoric times onward furnishes examples of burials. An excavation area, like that of Bab edh-Dhra located east of the Dead Sea, from the Early Bronze Age, antedates the Hebrew Patriarchs and shows the custom of placing the body in a shaft tomb cut into the rock into which were placed knives, spears, and a few clay vessels to accompany the dead. Later Palestinian periods also had other types of burials. In late Judaism, to bury the dead was considered an act of piety (Tob. 1:17; 2:3-10).

The experience of death was "to go the way of all the earth" (Josh. 23:14; 1 Kings 2:2); "to be gathered unto one's people" (Gen. 15:15; 25:8; 35:29; 49:29, 33; Num. 20:24, 26; 31:2; Deut. 32:50); "to sleep with one's fathers" (1 Kings 2:10; 11:21; 2 Kings 20:21); or to go to one's "eternal home" (Eccles. 12:5).

At death the spirit departed from the body; the body returned to the earth: "You are dust and to dust you shall return" (Gen. 3:19; Job 34:14-15). The spirit (*ruah*) returned to God who gave it (Eccles. 12:7). However, one also spoke of the *nephesh* departing at the time of death: "Her soul (*nephesh*) was departing (for she died)" (Gen. 35:18). Jonah can pray that his *nephesh* be taken from him (Jon. 4:3). The live person is a "living being" (*nephesh chayyah*; Gen. 1:20, 24, 30; 2:7; 9:12, 15-16); but the corpse can be spoken of as a *nephesh met*—a dead person (Lev. 21:11; Num. 6:6; 19:13). When God withdraws their breath (*ruah*), his creatures die (Ps. 104:29; cf. 146:4). These and similar cases show that neither *ruah* nor *nephesh* is a complete equivalent to the ideas the English reader attaches to the word "soul."

Neither the Old Testament nor the New Testament is materialistic: Daniel is grieved in his spirit within (Dan. 7:15). Although Samson can pray that his *nephesh* die with the Philistines (Judg. 16:30), *nephesh* in a case of this sort means "person" and stands for the personal pronoun.

Neither Testament encourages the idea of "soul sleeping." Though the dead are said to be asleep some twenty times in the Old Testament (cf. Job 14:12; Dan. 12:2), and while death in the New Testament is often compared to sleep (Mk. 5:39; 1 Thess. 5:10), this usage is euphemistic to avoid the harsh reality of the finality of death. It is comparable in force to our own phrase, "He passed away." Jesus contrasted the sleep of rest and the sleep of death (Jn. 11:11-14).[2]

SHEOL

The Hebrews envisioned the dead as going to a place they called *Sheol*. This word occurs sixty-six times in the Old Testament and is always a feminine noun that regularly is used without the definite article. It occurs in the Semitic languages other than Hebrew only as a loan word from Hebrew. Its etymology remains a debated question. One effort connects it with the verb *sha'al* meaning "to ask" and then conjectures that in its pagan background it had a connection with consulting the

[2]Tertullian asked, "Shall we sleep between death and the judgment? Why, souls do not sleep even when men are alive. It is the province of bodies to sleep." The fortieth article of belief of the Church of England also condemns the soul-sleeping view.

dead—a practice forbidden in the Old Testament (Deut. 18:11; 1 Chron. 10:13; Is. 8:19). Other scholars have attempted to trace *Sheol* to *sho'al* which means "hollow."

Sheol was envisioned as being beneath the earth so that one spoke of going down to Sheol (Gen. 37:35; 42:38; Is. 14:11, 15; Ezek. 31:15). One spoke of the depths of Sheol (Deut. 32:22; Ps. 86:13; 88:6); a descent there is set opposite an ascent into heaven (Ps. 139:8; Is. 14:14-15). The earth swallows Korah and his group as they go down to Sheol (Num. 16:30, 33). A narrow escape from death is to be brought up from the pit (Jon. 2:6; cf. Ps. 116:3). Amos speaks of the theoretical possibility of digging into Sheol (Amos 9:2; cf. Ps. 139:8).

The King James scholars created confusion for the English reader by translating *sheol* as "the grave" in thirty-one instances and as "hell" in thirty-one. Hell originally meant "hollow," but it has shifted to a much more sinister meaning in the past four hundred years. The King James scholars may have been attempting to distinguish the place of the righteous from that of the wicked.

One can speak of the worm and of Sheol in the same description (Job 17:13-16); nevertheless, Sheol is clearly to be distinguished from the grave (*qebher*; Gen. 23:4, etc.). Even the unburied go down to Sheol (Is. 14:19-20). Jacob thought the beasts had devoured Joseph, yet he expected to go to him in Sheol (Gen. 37:35). Moses was gathered to his people and was buried in Moab (Deut. 34:5-6); yet Miriam had been buried in the wilderness, Aaron on Mt. Hor, and his mother who made the ark of bulrushes likely had been buried in the brickfields of Egypt. Moses (Deut. 31:16), David, Ahaz, and Manasseh are all said to lie down with their fathers; yet none of them was buried in the family grave. There are also the statements, "He slept with his fathers and was buried" (1 Kings 14:31; 2 Kings 8:24; 2 Chron. 12:16), or "He slept with his fathers and they buried him" (1 Kings 15:8; 2 Kings 13:9; 2 Chron. 26:23). Samuel, when called up by the witch of Endor, predicts that Saul and his sons would be with him the next day. Yet their bodies were nailed to a wall in Bethshan and later their bones were burned (1 Sam. 28:13-19; 31:8-13). Samuel and these people were not together in the grave. The ASV attempted a correction of the confusion of the grave and Sheol by merely transliterating Hebrew letters to create the English word "Sheol."

The "nether world" (Ezek. 26:20; 31:14) and "the pit" (*bor*; Ps. 28:1; 88:4, 6; Is. 14:15; 38:18; Ezek. 32:18) are in some passages alternate designations for Sheol. *Bor* (the pit) in other settings is a cistern suitable for water storage which also could be used for holding a prisoner. Joseph and Jeremiah were imprisoned in cisterns. Other alternate words for Sheol are *shachath* (pit; Job 33:18; Ps. 16:10; 30:9; Is. 38:17; 51:14; Jon. 2:6) and *'abhaddon* (Job 26:6; 28:22; Ps. 88:11; Prov. 15:11; 27:20).

Sheol may be thought of in the figure of a city with gates (Job 38:17; Is. 38:10; Ps. 9:13; 107:18) or as a monster with insatiable appetite ready to devour (Prov. 1:12; 27:20; 30:15f.; Is. 5:14; Hab. 2:5) The psalmist laments, "Our bones are scattered at the mouth of Sheol" (Ps. 141:7). For the dead, Sheol is as a pasture for sheep with death as their shepherd (Ps. 49:14). Sheol is personified in Hos. 13:14. The way to Sheol is a way of no return (Job 7:10; 10:21; 16:22; 20:9); the living are eventually to go to the dead there (2 Sam. 12:23).

Sheol is a region dark and deep (Ps. 88:6) a region of chaos and gloom where light is darkness (Job 10:20-21). One looked upon the experience of going there with dread (Ps. 88:4) rather than with hopeful expectation. Hezekiah gave expression to these forebodings in his song which is connected with his recovery from illness (Is. 38:18). To be cut off from the living before one's time and sent down to Sheol is considered the direst doom (Ps. 78:18-20).

In a few scanty descriptions of conditions in Sheol which we have, it is a place to which all the dead go without division into rich and poor, righteous and wicked. One of the four things that never says "enough" (Prov. 30:16), Sheol is the house appointed for all living (Job 30:23); it is the "land of forgetfulness" (Ps. 88:12) where one does not know what happens in the upper world (Job 14:12). It is a place of silence (Ps. 94:17; 115:17) where one does not praise God (Ps. 6:5; 30:9; 88:10-12; 115:17) or hope for his faithfulness (Is. 38:18). There is no work, thought, knowledge, or wisdom in Sheol (Eccles. 9:10). A threefold distinction marks out the heavens as the Lord's, the earth as man's, and Sheol for the dead (Ps. 115:16-18).

Nevertheless, existence in Sheol is a conscious existence. While certain passages speak of the *nephesh* as though it went to Sheol (Ps. 16:10; 30:3; 86:13; 89:48; 94:17; Prov. 23:14) and speak of recovery from near death as the *nephesh* being brought back from Sheol, it is neither *nephesh* nor *ruah* that describes the inhabitants there. Rather, they are "shades" (*rephaim*; Job 26:5; Prov. 2:18; 21:16; Ps. 88:10; Is. 14:9; 26:14), that is, weak ones. Contrasted with earthly cares and sufferings, for one in distress like Job, Sheol is a place of "rest." "There the wicked cease from troubling and there the weary are at rest. There the prisoners are at ease together; they hear not the voice of the taskmaster. The small and the great are there, and the slave is free from his master"

(Job 3:17-19).

In a taunt song the prophet Isaiah presents a picture of the descent of the King of Babylon to Sheol (Is. 14:4ff.). The shades already there rise up to greet the new arrival. Those who were kings of the nations rise from their thrones and taunt the king now that he has become as weak as they have.

Ezekiel in another taunt speaks of Egypt going down to the nether world, down to the pit. The uncircumcised are there; Assyria, Elam, Meshek and Tubal, Edom and the princes of the North—are all there. The warriors are described as going down with their swords and shields (Ezek. 32:18-31).

Some scholars,[3] impressed by such a question as "Can the shades in Sheol praise thee?" (Ps. 88:10), have argued that Sheol is outside the concern of Jehovah. However, the psalmist elsewhere affirms that even the experience of Sheol cannot separate him from the Lord: "If I make my bed in Sheol, you are there" (Ps. 139:8). Sheol is naked before God (Job 26:6; Prov. 15:11), and his anger burns to its depths (Deut. 32:22). He brings down to Sheol and raises up (1 Sam. 2:6). "Though they dig into Sheol, from there my hand shall take them" (Amos 9:2). Nevertheless, it is stated that man cannot praise God there (Is. 38:18).

BETWEEN THE TESTAMENTS[4]

When the Septuagint translators sought for their nearest equivalent of Sheol, they selected *hadēs* (from

[3]R. H. Charles, *Eschatology* (New York: Schocken Books, 1963), pp. 35ff.

[4]See D. S. Russell, *The Method and Message of Jewish Apocalyptic* (Philadelphia, Pa.: Westminster Press, 1964), pp. 366ff.

the Greek word *idein*—to see) which means "the unseen realm." But what the Greeks had previously meant by Hades is not a complete equivalent to what the Hebrews meant by Sheol. Yet the term is fifty-nine times in the Greek Old Testament for Sheol and is a few times for other words, laying a basis for its usage in the New Testament.

In Qumran, Sheol was used in ways comparable to those seen in the Old Testament. Located in the depths of the earth,[5] Sheol is the dreaded place to which the dead go.[6] Childbirth may be compared to the pains of Sheol;[7] one in suffering may speak of his groaning being shut up in the chambers of Sheol;[8] and a recovery to health is being "redeemed from the pit, from the Sheol of *'abhaddon*."[9]

There is no one uniform idea about the intermediate state of the dead expressed in the intertestamental literature, and some of the sources present divergent views within themselves. In some sources both the righteous and the wicked go to Sheol (the Hadean world; Ecclus. 17:27-30; 41:1-4).[10] Sheol is a land of forgetfulness where men are more blessed than those who live in suffering here on earth.[11] There are those identified as "sinners" who insist that the fate of the righteous and the wicked are the same,[12] but the more general view is that there are different fates for the righteous and for the wicked. While both go to Sheol,[13] the choice of their fate there has

[5]QH 17:13.
[6]Ibid., 8:28; 9:4.
[7]Ibid., 3:9-10.
[8]Ibid., 10:33.
[9]Ibid., 3:19-20.
[10]1 Enoch 51; 4 Ez. 4:41; 7:32; 2 Bar. 21:23f.
[11]2 Bar. 11:5-7.
[12]1 En. 102:6-8, 11.
[13]2 Bar. 21:23; 23:5; 48:6; 52:2; 83:17.

been made in this life.

In 1 Enoch 22, written about 170 B.C., there is a description of a place, not underground but in the west, where four hollow places receive the spirits of the dead until the day of judgment. There is a place for the righteous, another for those martyred who demand vengeance on those who wronged them,[14] another for sinners who have met retribution in this life, and still another for those who have not. Elsewhere it speaks of the spirits of the righteous passing into happy dwelling places at the ends of the heavens.[15] The book says nothing of the spirit's passing to Hades.

That Sheol is an intermediate state—not a permanent one—for the righteous is expressed elsewhere (2 Macc. 7:9, 11, 14, 36-37).[16] At death the souls of the righteous enter "chambers" or "treasuries of souls" where they are to enjoy great quietness and are guarded by the angels of God.[17] At the time of judgment these chambers shall restore the souls that were committed to them.[18] After the judgment, the pit of torment appears opposite the place of refreshment, and the furnace of Gehenna is opposite the Paradise of delight.[19] Still another source speaks of places prepared in Sheol for the repose of souls until the final judgment.[20]

The idea that there is retribution in Sheol is ex-

[14]R. H. Charles, *The Book of Enoch* (Oxford, England: Clarendon Press, 1912), pp. 46-47. The author argues that this division is illogical and that in reality there should be only three divisions. This contention seems unnecessary.

[15]1 En. 39:3-8; cf. 41:2-4.

[16]Ibid., 51.

[17]4 Ez. 4:35; 7:95.

[18]Ibid., 7:32.

[19]Ibid., 7:32, 36.

[20]2 En. 58:4-6; 49:2.

pressed;[21] but that the wicked are raised to be punished seems unexpressed. There is tribulation,[22] and the wicked are slain.[23] In these sources Sheol approaches to being an equivalent to the concept of Gehenna.[24] It is a place of condemnation[25] and of darkness.[26]

Certain sources[27] present the view that the wicked after death enter immediately into eternal punishment in a region thought of as under the earth. 1 Enoch 39 represents the righteous dead as entering into a state of blessedness that seems to be in the vicinity of God; but at the end there is judgment and blessedness. In 2 Enoch 9f., where the place of the blessed and the place of the condemned is in the third heaven, nothing is said about whether inhabitants are already there at the time of the vision or whether the places are prepared only for their eventual use.

In Hellenistic Judaism, which subscribed to the immortality of the soul (as contrasted with the resurrection of the body), the souls of the righteous are in the hands of God and no evil can touch them (Wisd. 3:1ff.). The soul receives its fate immediately at death. Those who die as martyrs live with God as do Abraham, Isaac, and Jacob.[28] The patriarchs receive the martyrs;[29] that is, the patriarchs form a sort of community[30] to which the martyrs come. According to Josephus[31] the Essenes thought

[21]1 Enoch 22.
[22]Ibid., 103:7-8.
[23]Ibid., 99:11.
[24]Ibid., 63:8-10; 99:11; 103:7.
[25]Jub. 7:29; 22:22; 24:31.
[26]Ibid., 7:29.
[27]Ps. of Sol. 3:11ff.; 14:9; 15:10.
[28]4 Macc. 7:19.
[29]Ibid., 5:37.
[30]Apoc. Zephaniah 17:3.
[31]Josephus *War* 2.154ff.; *Antiquities* 18.18.

of the soul of the righteous at death taking its flight upward as though freed from prison to a place on the other side of the ocean.

While these various views are not in any sense normative for the Christian, they do reveal how manifold the background of beliefs was against which Jesus taught.

HADES

In New Testament thought where man is made up of body, soul, and spirit (1 Thess. 5:23), one disintegrates when he dies. A clear distinction is made between body and spirit (Rom. 8:10). The body apart from the spirit (*pneuma*) is dead (Jas. 2:26). When one is restored to life, the spirit returns (Lk. 8:55). The experience of dying is the yielding up of one's spirit (Mt. 27:50). Jesus committed his spirit into the hands of God and expired (Lk. 23:46). When put to death in the flesh, he was made alive in the spirit (1 Pet. 3:18). Stephen prays that Jesus will receive his spirit (Acts 7:59). On the other hand, to seek one's *psuchē* is to seek to kill him (Mt. 2:20); in dying one gives up the *psuchē* (Acts 5:5, 10; 12:23); his *psuchē* is required of him (Lk. 12:16-20); and when one is restored to life, he is said to have his *psuchē* in him (Acts 20:10).

A live person is at home in the body (2 Cor. 5:6-8); but one can be "out of the body" (2 Cor. 12:2-4); he can "put off this tabernacle" (2 Pet. 1:14-15; cf. Phil. 1:13-14). Though death is universal in scope (Rom. 5:12ff.), matters concerning the dead, such as burial, are treated as of secondary importance (Mt. 8:21-22). One does not fear him who can kill only the body (Mt. 10:28).

Death for the righteous is not viewed as an unpleasant prospect: "Blessed are the dead that die in the Lord"

(Rev. 14:13). It is being received into "eternal habitations" (Lk. 16:9). Death is a falling asleep (Acts 7:60; 1 Cor. 15:20; 1 Thess. 4:13); but this euphemism is not at all to espouse Sadducean views that the soul dies with the body.[32] Jesus argued that God is not the God of the dead but of the living. Abraham, Isaac, and Jacob in some condition were alive (Mt. 22:32). Abraham saw Jesus' day (Jn. 8:56). All are alive to God (Lk. 20:38). Moses and Elijah can be brought back for the transfiguration scene (Mt. 17:1ff.). Paul definitely envisions the possibility of being out of the body in a conscious condition (2 Cor. 12:1ff.).

The term *hadēs* (Latin, *infernus*) occurs ten times in the New Testament with the instances dispersed in only four out of the twenty-seven books.[33] In the New Testament, "Hades" never designates the place of final punishment of the wicked after the judgment; for that state the term *geenna* (Latin, *gehenna*) is used twelve times. Unfortunately, the KJV obliterates for the English reader this uniform distinction by using "hell" for the rendering of both of these terms.

Hades, serving in the New Testament only an interim purpose, receives the souls at death (Lk. 16:23) and yields them up at the resurrection (Rev. 20:13). The resurrection constitutes its end, for the last enemy to be destroyed is death (1 Cor. 15:26). In certain passages where there is a personification, Death and Hades, along with the wicked, are cast into the lake of fire (Rev. 19:20; 20:10; 14f.).

Hades may also be used metaphorically. As the king of Babylon is taunted with a descent into Sheol (Is. 14:13,

[32]Ibid., *Antiquities* 18.16.

[33]The *Textus Receptus* has an additional case in 1 Cor. 15:55 which is more correctly *thanatos*, "death."

15), so Capernaum is threatened with being brought down to Hades (Mt. 11:23; Lk. 10:15)—the lowest known depth (cf. Deut. 32:22; Job 11:8; 26:6; Is. 7:11; 57:9). This figurative expression implies that Capernaum will be utterly overthrown. Only in this saying is Hades not directly associated with death in the New Testament.

Metaphorically, Hades may be conceived of as a prison which has gates (Mt. 16:18). The expression "gates of Hades" parallels the Old Testament phrase "gates of Sheol" (Job 17:16; 38:17; Is. 38:10)[34] and continues the view found in the apocryphal literature where a person about to die is said to be standing at the very gates of Hades (3 Macc. 5:51). God is considered to have control over it: "For thou hast authority over life and death, and leadest down to the gates of Hades and bringest up again" (Wisd. 16:13). While it is popular to see in Jesus' statement made to Peter (alluded to above) a promise that all the forces of evil cannot overcome the church, the statement likely refers to Jesus' own death. Death will not frustrate his plans (cf. Acts 2:27, 31). In the resurrection he won a victory over Hades, robbing death of its sting (1 Cor. 15:55). Jesus has the keys to this Hadean prison (Rev. 1:18).[35] Though Death and Hades (personified) kill a fourth of mankind (Rev. 6:8), Hades will give up its dead for judgment (Rev. 20:13) before Death and Hades themselves are cast into the lake of fire (Rev. 20:14). In the New Heaven and Earth, death will be no more (Rev. 21:4).

Our clearest description of existence in Hades is in the story of the rich man and Lazarus (Lk. 16:19ff.). While the parable is designed to warn against the selfish life and is not primarily designed to inform us about the

[34]Cf. Ps. of Sol. 16:2.
[35]Cf. T. Levi 18:10.

state of the dead, it does presuppose that there is a distinct place or condition of abode for the righteous and for the wicked. As Jesus' promise to the dying thief implies (Lk. 23:43), this story suggests immediate entrance into a new conscious state. Those there have taken nothing of what they had with them. The misery of the one and the comfort of the other is obvious in the story. The rich man knows where he is, knows where Lazarus is, and knows that he yet has brothers back upon earth and he is concerned about them. No character changes or personality changes have been made. "I" is still the "I" he was when back on earth and is not somebody else. He did not get away from himself. Memory is still there. The judgment has not yet taken place; he is not in hell. Yet he and Lazarus are separated from each other by an uncrossable chasm. "Abraham's bosom" (the word is used both in the singular and in the plural in the story) is not a synonym for Paradise; but to recline on Abraham's bosom one would need to be in Paradise where Abraham is. We need not at this time solve the debate over whether the picture is that of a father receiving a child into his lap (cf. Jn. 1:18) or whether we are to envision a banquet scene (cf. Jn. 13:23) in which the invited guest reclines nearest the host.

Both Peter and Paul assume that all souls (*psuchae*) go to Hades. From Acts 2:27, 31 (quoting Ps. 16:10), we learn that Jesus, at death, went to Hades: "Thou wilt not abandon my soul to Hades nor let thy Holy One see corruption" (cf. Acts 13:35-37). Elsewhere it is said that Jesus descended into the lower part of the earth (Eph. 4:9) which must mean the underworld.

Yet when he spoke to the thief, Jesus spoke of going with him—not to heaven, but—to Paradise that day (Lk. 23:43). The promise is, "Today you shall be with me in

Paradise." The obvious antithesis in the passage is between the indefinite "when you come in your kingdom" used by the thief, and "Today you shall be with me" used by Jesus. There is nothing to be said textually or logically for the effort, made by different punctuation, to connect "Today" with the verb "I say" to make "I say unto you today . . . ." While the Curetonian Syriac Version,[36] Theophylact of the Church Fathers,[37] and now the Jehovah's Witnesses in the New World Translation propose this punctuation, such punctuation turns a pointed contrast into a superfluous self-evident statement. In other formula quotations using "verily" in the New Testament, that which follows belongs not with the formula but with the statement which comes after. Henry Alford characterized the effort to repunctuate as "surely something worse than silly."[38] Adam Clarke saw it as "most feeble and worthless criticism";[39] and most current commentaries do not even notice the possibility. Plummer said, "To take this (*sēmeron*) with *legō* robs it of almost all its force. When taken with what follows, it is full of meaning."[40]

"Paradise" is a word of Persian origin meaning an enclosed park[41] and is so used in the Septuagint (Neh. 2:8; Eccles. 2:5; Song 4:13). It is often used for the Garden of Eden (Gen. 2:8ff.; etc.). But then it is also used three

[36]Metzger, *A Textual Commentary on the Greek New Testament*, pp. 181-82.

[37]Cited in J. J. van Oosterzee, *The Gospel According to Luke*, 6th ed. (Edinburgh, Scotland: T. & T. Clark, 1870), p. 377.

[38]Henry Alford, *The Greek New Testament*, rev. E. F. Harrison (Chicago, Ill.: Moody Press, 1958), p. 661.

[39]Adam Clarke, *The New Testament of Our Lord and Saviour Jesus Christ* (New York: Abingdon-Cokesbury Press, n.d.), 1:497.

[40]A. Plummer, *A Critical and Exegetical Commentary on the Gospel According to St. Luke* (Edinburgh, Scotland: T. & T. Clark, 1956), p. 545.

[41]Xenophon *Anabasis* 1.2.7; 2.4.14; etc.

times in the New Testament. By Paul it is an alternate designation for the third heaven (2 Cor. 12:3);[42] it is used in the Book of Revelation (2:7) for the location of the tree of life available to him who overcomes; and then it is used in our passage (Lk. 23:43).

In late Jewish sources, Paradise is variously conceived so that appeal to them does little to solve the problem concerning its location. Sometimes it is on earth, sometimes it is in heaven, and sometimes between heaven and earth. In some of the Jewish apocalypses such as 4 Ezra (7:36, 123; 8:52) written near the end of the first century and in such later works as 2 Bar. 51:10-11 and 2 En. 8ff.,[43] Paradise also designates the place of the final reward of the righteous.

The important issue in the whole consideration of the state of the dead is that of whether or not Paradise in the Lord's promise to the thief is used in the same way that it is used by Paul in 2 Cor. 12:3. Many contend that it is; but this position faces the difficulty that according to Acts 2:27, 31, Jesus went to Hades at death rather than to heaven. Because of this difficulty, from the chain of evidence we have presented, we deduce the idea that Paradise in Jesus' statement is a designation for a part of Hades. We then connect Paradise with the parable to deduce that this is where Abraham and Lazarus must be. That it was not heaven also follows from the fact that after three days in Hades Jesus said to the woman, "Touch me not for I have not yet ascended to my Father" (Jn. 20:17). God's dwelling obviously is in heaven (2 Chron. 6:33). Jesus had not gone to heaven; Hades in the Lukan passage is not in heaven; Paradise in the thief

[42]Cf. Apoc. Mos. 40:3; 2 En. 8:1ff.

[43]G. H. Box, *The Ezra-Apocalypse* (London: Isaac Pitman & Sons, 1912), pp. 195-97.

passage is not in heaven.

Jesus' story contains no name for the section of Hades where the rich man is. The noun "Tartarus," often used to describe the place of the wicked dead, does not occur in the Bible at all. That it can be used to describe a part of Hades is a triple deduction, partly dependent on Greek ideas,[44] partly dependent upon the Jewish apocalypses,[45] and partly dependent upon a statement of 2 Pet. 2:4 (cf. Jude 6) where a verb *tartaroun* (meaning to imprison in Tartarus) occurs in the aorist participial form. The free paraphrase rendering of the RSV is:

> For if God did not spare angels when they sinned, but cast them into hell [*tartarosas*] and committed them to pits of nether gloom to be kept until the judgment . . . .

Reasoning from the logic that wicked angels and wicked men are kept in the same place and from the fact that Greeks did use Tartarus for the nether world, it is the conviction of many that this term may legitimately be used for the intermediate state of the wicked. There is no further evidence.

THE CHURCH FATHERS

Already in the second Christian century the view that the righteous dead went to Hades was firmly held in the church. Justin Martyr said, "The souls of the pious remain in a better place, while those of the unjust and

[44]Plato *Phaedo* 113 E; Homer *Iliad* 1.13; etc.; Josephus *Apion* 2.2.40.

[45]1 En. 20:2; Sib. 1:126-29.

wicked in a worse, waiting for the time of judgment."[46] Irenaeus said, "For as the Lord 'went away in the midst of the shadow of death,' where the souls of the dead were, yet afterwards arose in the body, and after the resurrection was taken up [*into heaven*], it is manifest that the souls of his disciples also, upon whose account the Lord underwent these things, shall go away into the invisible place allotted to them by God, and there remain until the resurrection, awaiting that event . . . as our Master, therefore, did not at once depart, taking flight [*to heaven*], but awaited the time of our resurrection prescribed by the Father, which had also shown forth through Jonas, and rising again after three days was taken up [*to heaven*], so ought we to await the time of our resurrection prescribed by God and foretold by the prophets, and so, rising, be taken up, as many as the Lord shall account worthy of this [*privilege*]."[47] Similar views are expressed by Tertullian: "For no one, on becoming absent from the body, is at once a dweller in the presence of the Lord, except by the prerogative of martyrdom, he gains a lodging in Paradise, not in the lower regions."[48] Similiar views are dominant throughout the patristic period.

THE RIGHTEOUS DEAD IN HEAVEN?

An alternate position to consider is that which contends that the righteous go to heaven at the time of death instead of to Hades. Such an idea ordinarily accompanied by the idea that the wicked are cast directly into

[46]Justin *Dialogue* 5.
[47]Irenaeus *Adv. Haer.* 5.31.2 (ANF 1:560).
[48]Tertullian *On the Resurrection of the Flesh* 45 (ANF 3:476).

hell[49] is older than Christianity.[50] In the Book of Jubilees, in a passage which deals with immortality rather than with resurrection, the bones of the righteous rest in the earth, but their spirits shall have much joy.[51] In 2 Enoch the wicked are cast into torment (10:1), but the righteous are taken to Paradise (42:3; etc.). Abraham is said to have been taken to heaven when he died.[52] Paradise is a place of life everlasting,[53] and the souls of the blessed enjoy foods and blessedness forever.[54] Certain other pseudepigraphical writings depict Hades as the place only for the wicked dead. According to Josephus, the Sadducees denied rewards and punishments in Hades;[55] the Pharisees believed that the souls of both the righteous and the wicked went to Hades;[56] but Josephus himself seems to have believed that the righteous went to a heavenly existence[57] and that only the wicked went to Hades.[58] Certain of the rabbis (the Amoraim) of the post-Christian period subscribed to a similar view.[59]

Some scholars have argued that Abraham and Lazarus were not in Hades at all, but that the term "Hades" of the biblical passage describes only the condition of the rich man. The issue turns on whether there are two divisions in Hades or whether the distinction is to be

[49] 1 Enoch 103.

[50] Paul Volz, *Die Eschatologie der judischen Gemeinde im neutestamentlichen Zeitalter* (Tübingen, West Germany: J. C. B. Mohr, 1934), p. 20.

[51] Jub. 23:31.

[52] T. Abraham 7:16f.

[53] Ibid., 20.

[54] Apoc. Abraham 21.

[55] Josephus *War* 2.165.

[56] Ibid., *Antiquities* 18.14; *War* 2.163.

[57] Ibid., *War* 3.374f.

[58] Ibid., 3.375.

[59] *T.B. Shabbath* 152b; G. F. Moore, *Judaism* (Cambridge: Harvard University Press, 1946), 2:287ff.

made between where Abraham is and Hades where the rich man is. I have assumed in the previous argument that Abraham is in Hades.[60]

Assuming the validity of the interpretation we have given to the story of the rich man and Lazarus, and of that given to the promise made to the thief, it seems obvious that Jesus rejected the view that the righteous go directly to heaven. The account of Jesus' own experience in death as given in the Book of Acts is also a rejection of this idea. His soul went to Hades (Acts 2:27, 31), and though in Hades three days, he had not yet ascended to the Father (Jn. 20:17). The promise of the Lord to his disciples was that he was going to prepare a place for them and that he would come again and receive them unto himself (Jn. 14:1-3). The fair import of these words is that they must wait until he comes for this experience.

WAS HADES FOR THE RIGHTEOUS TERMINATED AT THE RESURRECTION OF JESUS?

It has been argued by F. G. Allen[61] and Eugene S. Smith[62] that a significant change in the state of the righteous dead took place at the resurrection of Jesus. Beginning from the passage, "He led captivity captive" (Eph. 4:8), considering that Paradise with Paul is in the

[60]S. D. F. Salmon, in *The Christian Doctrine of Immortality* (Edinburgh, Scotland: T. & T. Clark, 1895), pp. 349-52, argues that Jesus' use of Hades and Paradise is inadequate to prove that he taught an intermediate state.

[61]F. G. Allen, "The State of the Righteous Dead," *The Old Paths Pulpit* (Nashville, Tenn.: Gospel Advocate Publishing Co., 1940), pp. 272-90.

[62]Eugene S. Smith, *Eternal Home* (Dallas, Tex.: Gospel Broadcast Press, n.d.), p. 32.

third heaven (2 Cor. 12:3), and noticing that passages after the resurrection of Jesus do not allude to the righteous being in Hades, Allen argued that the resurrection of Jesus emptied Hades of the righteous, took Paradise to heaven, and abolished that part of Hades. According to Allen's contention, since that time the righteous at death have gone directly to heaven.

This position is, of course, older than these men. Tertullian knew certain people whom he insists should be kept at arm's length who made a like contention. He denies their case, pointing out that only the souls of the martyrs are seen under the altar in Revelation 6. He therefore believes that only the martyrs go directly to Paradise, but that others of the righteous are detained in Hades until the resurrection.[63]

That the righteous go directly to heaven was advocated by some Reformers,[64] is advocated by certain of the notable creeds,[65] is argued for by Hodge,[66] and is held to by many current denominations.[67]

[63]Tertullian *A Treatise on the Soul* 55 (ANF 3:231); *On the Resurrection of the Flesh* 43 (ANF 3:576).

[64]John Calvin, *Institutes* ii. 16.8-12. Cf. Heinrich Quistorph, *Calvin's Doctrine of the Last Things* (London: Lutterworth Press, 1955), pp. 81ff.

[65]*Westminster Confession of Faith*, Article 32: "The souls of the righteous, being made perfect in holiness, are received into the highest heavens, where they behold the face of God in light and glory, waiting for the full redemption of their bodies: and the souls of the wicked are cast into hell, where they remain in torments and utter darkness, reserved to the judgment of the great day." *Heidelberg Catechism*, Q. 57: "That not only my soul, after this life, shall be immediately taken up to Christ its Head, but also that this my body, raised by the power of Christ, shall again be united with my soul, and made like the glorious body of Christ."

[66]Charles Hodge, *Systematic Theology* (Grand Rapids, Mich.: Wm. B. Eerdmans Publishing Co., 1952), 3:724ff.

[67]Karel Hanhart, *The Intermediate State of the Dead in the New Testament* (Franeker: T. Weyer, n.d.), pp. 248ff., argues that the intermediate state is not the object of investigation or speculation.

In response to this case, we contend that the passage, "He led captivity captive" (Eph. 4:8) likely refers only to Jesus' victory over death. There is no compelling reason to read into it an emptying of Hades of the righteous in order to establish a position. No passage specifically states that Jesus' death affected the state of the dead in the time prior to the resurrection.

Though we have already noticed that the term "Hades" does not occur in any New Testament epistle, I know none among us who would deduce from that fact that the wicked dead are not in Hades. Let this also be a caution against arguing from silence about the condition of the righteous dead. As far as I know, except for materialists and "soul sleepers," there is no debate over whether the wicked dead go to Hades.

Certain other New Testament passages have also been thought to suggest the immediate transfer of the righteous dead or a part of them to heaven. Stephen sees the heavens open up and the Son of man standing at the right hand of God and prays, "Lord Jesus, receive my spirit" (Acts 7:59). While here in the body, we are absent from the Lord, but to die is to be at home with him (2 Cor. 5:8). Paul longs to depart to be with Christ (Phil. 1:23); those who have fallen asleep will the Lord bring with him; the living will be caught up; and "so shall we ever be with the Lord" (1 Thess. 4:17). At his coming we shall see him as he is and shall be like him (1 Jn. 3:2). In the Apocalypse John sees a vision in heaven in which under the altar are souls (*psuchae*) of those who have been slain for the word of God (Rev. 6:9ff.; 7:9ff.; 15:2ff.). The scene of chapter 6 assumes that the judgment has not yet taken place. Of these verses it is often argued that the righteous, or at least the martyrs, go directly to heaven at death rather than going to Hades.

That these expectations are actually in tension with the view that the dead are in Hades is true only after two assumptions are made, neither of which is compelling. First is the assumption that our concept of time is valid in the intermediate world. Our finite mind dwells upon the long lapse of time between death and the resurrection. But with the Lord one day is as a thousand years (2 Pet. 3:8). Why then should we impose our time assumption upon the dead? The statement, "It is appointed unto men to die once, and after this comes the judgment" (Heb. 9:27), if pressed in isolation could be made to teach immediate judgment; but we know from other Scriptures that such cannot be. The above-mentioned considerations dull the argument that Paul did not expect to spend a long time in the intermediate state. There is an intermediate existence in Paul's thought. Paul's goal is to attain to the resurrection of the dead (Phil. 3:10-11), but he clearly distinguishes between departing "to be with Christ" (Phil. 1:23) and the receiving of his ultimate reward—"the crown of life which the Lord, the righteous judge, will give to me in that day" (2 Tim. 4:8). That is precisely when Jesus taught that men would be rewarded—"at the resurrection of the just" (Lk. 14:12-14). Are we to assume that Paul's existence in this intermediate state is different from that experienced by Christ himself between his death and resurrection? Is it different from that promised the thief (Lk. 23:43)?

The second assumption is spatial. We regularly assume that Hades is spatial and that it must be located in the nether world; then we deduce that it cannot be spoken of as "being with Christ." If Hades could be conceived of as a state in which the dead have communion with Christ and God, it would relieve the tension between the Hades concept and Paul's statement about departing to be with

Christ.

Looking at the other side of our problem, the position that the righteous go directly to heaven is also not without its own problems. The promise of the Lord which we have already noticed is that he would take the disciples to himself when he returns (Jn. 14:1-3). Upon this promise, one would expect to have to await that event for this experience. Furthermore, even after the resurrection—the time at which Jesus is supposed to have emptied Hades of the righteous—Peter declared, "For David did not ascend into the heavens" (Acts 2:34).[68] It is not solely David's body which is being discussed in the passage. His body saw corruption. The argument would seem to make clear that David was still in Hades. How shall we exclude him from the righteous allegedly taken to heaven?

CONCLUSION

From all of these considerations we believe that all the dead go to the Hadean world. The righteous are "with Christ," are in "Abraham's bosom," are in "Paradise" or "under the altar"—all of which show a nearness to God. At the end when death is overcome, Death and Hades give up their dead for judgment and are themselves destroyed. There are then rewards and punishments as the Lord's justice and mercy shall determine.

[68]F. F. Bruce, *The Acts of the Apostles* (Grand Rapids, Mich.: Wm. B. Eerdmans Publishing Co., 1960), p. 95.

Indexes

HEBREW WORD INDEX

GREEK WORD INDEX

LATIN WORD INDEX

SCRIPTURE INDEX

OLD TESTAMENT

APOCRYPHA INDEX

PSEUDEPIGRAPHA INDEX

SUBJECT INDEX